1

Parish and People

Richard Broad
M.A., Oxon., Dip.Ed., Oxon

Dunkeswell, Devon

First published in 1994 by

Richard Broad
M.A., Oxon., Dip.Ed., Oxon
Tencery Cottage
Dunkeswell
Honiton
Devon
EX14 0QZ

ISBN 0 9523829 0 3

Printed by Axxent Ltd,
99-101, St Leonards Road, Windsor, Berkshire, SL4 3BZ

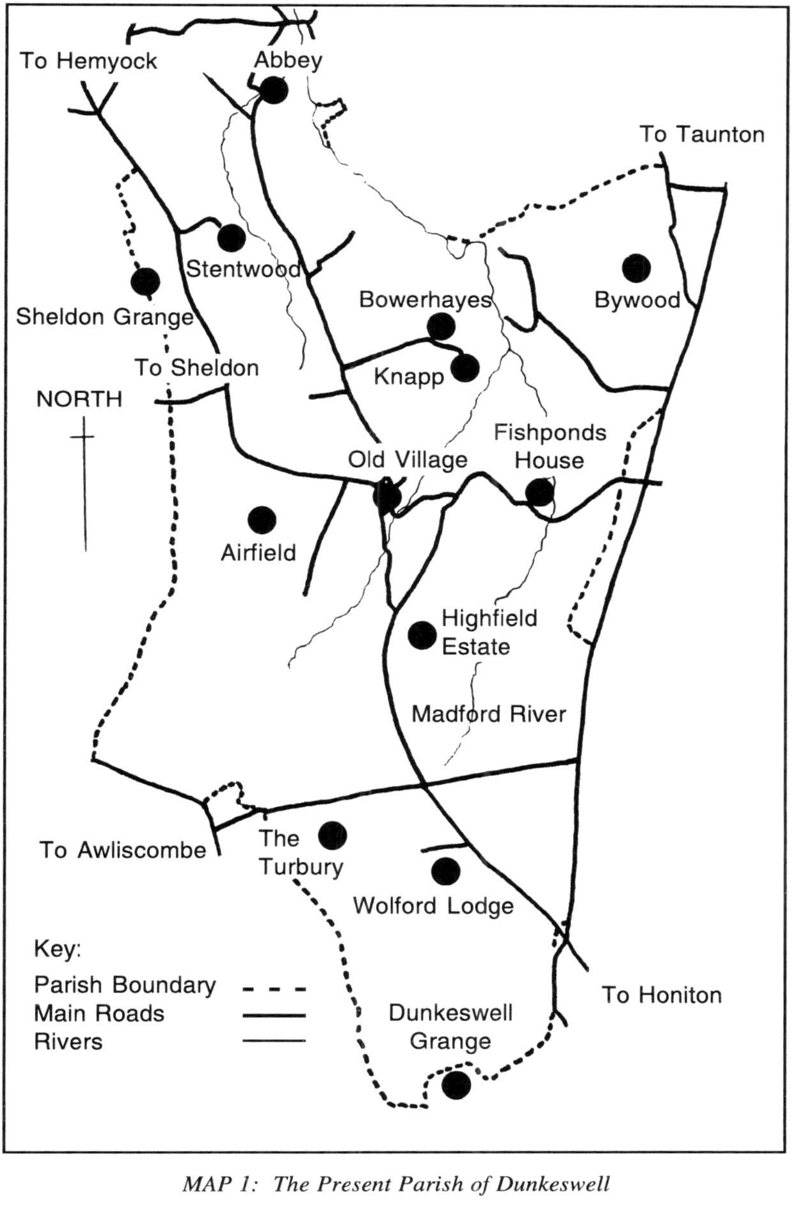

MAP 1: The Present Parish of Dunkeswell

To Cynthia
for her encouragement, understanding and help,
especially with the proof-reading.

CONTENTS

Chapter 1

Introduction

The Blackdown Hills are often obscured by mist and the history of Dunkeswell is obscured by the fog of uncertainty. Some of the historical records of the village have been lost, through age or mischance, through the action of Henry VIII's Commissioners who carried out the Dissolution of Dunkeswell Abbey or in the destruction by German bombers of some of Exeter's documents in 1942, and through the failure to keep them properly in the first place. Even the Police records are very scanty. Thus, any attempt to write the history is bound to be somewhat unbalanced. Dunkeswell has never been a fashionable village and writers and artists did not come to record its charm or interest as they went, for example, to Broadhembury or Sidmouth. For parts of its life, Dunkeswell was in the shadow of greater neighbours, particularly the powerful Cistercian Abbey; the social, military and imperial fame of the Simcoes lay at Wolford, on the edge of the Parish, and it was to the heights above the village that 5,000 American Naval personnel came in the 1940s and drank the "Royal Oak" dry of beer. Great national movements, from the Roman invasion to the agrarian riots of the early C19th, left Dunkeswell, again, on the fringe of events. Trading, agricultural, social, transport and administrative factors pulled Dunkeswell in two directions. The tenth century unit of administration was the Hundred of Hemyock and villagers looked across the Blackdowns to that larger settlement for supplies and trade and, later, to send milk to the Culm Valley Light Railway terminus there; on the other hand, they looked down to the late C13th fairs and markets at Awliscombe and Broadhembury and the flourishing market town of Honiton, with its wool and lace industries and road and rail links for larger markets, the Magistrates' Court and the C19th Workhouse, and along the old Roman road to Exeter, to the more august units of administration, the Cathedral, main law courts, gaol and County Council.

Yet, Dunkeswell very much had its own character and cherished its independence and relative isolation; it enjoyed its years of comparative fame and wider attention but remained a closely knit community, looking after its own people and its own problems. It did not suffer great swings of population and it has been only in the last few years that its new housing estate has caused a marked increase in inhabitants within the Parish, opening up the village to often urbanised newcomers and giving more opportunities to its own people. It speaks well of the old village that it was able to cope so capably with both the influx of American personnel in the last War and the newcomers of the 1980s and 1990s, being ready to welcome yet keeping its own identity. With the creation of industrial estates on the airfield area and with its position between the M5 and the A30, Dunkeswell has been opened to much traffic, ill suited to the narrow and idiosyncratic road system. The closure of many of the village shops and facilities, in common with those of other villages, and the growth of car ownership have made the inhabitants become much more outward looking for the basic things of life and for recreational pursuits and they not may fully recognise the history around them or their long links with the past; those links cannot be lost under new building and an increasingly busy life. On Highfield Estate there are hints as to the history of the village, particularly in the names of its roads; Jenwood Road and Le Marchant Close, Catalina Close and Simcoe Way, Tower Way and Kennedy Way; and the Estate looks down on the older settlement. It is part of the challenge of a constantly evolving history that a new community life will establish itself based upon the tradition of the past.

Chapter 2

Dunkeswell of the Blackdowns

It is certain that Dunkeswell has always been in Devon, although a legal document, dated 1st October, 1817, from Messrs Rowland and Others to Mr.Henry Dark, refers to the "Demesne of a cottage (Mansell's) in Dunkeswell in the County of Somerset". Even now, however, Devon County Council happily addresses letters to Dunkerswell and, until recently, that extra "r" was painted on some of the County's signposts. The name is well known in many parts of the United States and Air Wing 7 veterans can be forgiven for their versions of the name of the very small village in which they were stationed; perhaps they simply carried on the English tradition of random spelling which finally gave the modern form, Dunkeswell. That great work of William the Conqueror, Domesday Book, had the Latinised form, Doduceswilla; the Exchequer Records of 1100 rendered it Doducheswelle and the Feet of Fines (the bottom copy of the finis or end of a dispute over land, which went to the Treasury) opted for Danekewell in 1198. The Book of Fees actually got it right in 1234 but the Patent Rolls of 1265 made it Donecwell and the Tax Record of 1291 became more convoluted, with Donekyswille. Even the Diocesan Registers at Exeter proved uncertain. More local spelling wobbled all over the place, from Dunekeswell and Dunuceswielle to Dunnuc's Well and the name still tends to defeat those at the other end of a telephone line.Its meaning is not altogether clear, either. Perhaps, it referred to the Well of Dark Water, Dwn being the Welsh for dark and Donn the Irish version, or, more likely, the Well of Clear Water which attracted the first settlers. Other interpretations have been the Well of the Dead Oak and Dunnuc's Well, perhaps after the head of the Saxon family that came first to the site. The large number of Dunnocks (Prunella Modularis), the grey headed, thin-billed and jingling-warbling hedge sparrows, might possibly have given their name to the Well of the Dunnocks. Parts of the Parish have names which seem elusive, too, particularly the area of Rough Grey Bottom; over the centuries, it evolved from Ruffegereihy of 1253 to the

Roughegrey Common of 1550 and probably came from the family name of Eleanor Rufferegerey with the addition of its location, by a river. One part of the Parish is still known, simply, as Bottom. In another part, Hokederis turned to Hockedrys and then to Hookedrise; the Old English, Hocedan-hrisan, meant a bent piece of land covered with brushwood. At least, in those names, there is a linguistic clue; in a word such as Tencery, speculation must play a part. There was a medieval tax, Tencerie, by which land was held from a landlord, probably Dunkeswell Abbey, which owned much of the village, or it may have been a corruption of Penitentiary, a place away from the Abbey in which a monk served out a penance imposed by his Abbot. Such speculation is the fascination of History!

Dunkeswell sits on the southern edge of the Blackdown Hills, in an area of great beauty, where the work of the farmer complements the work of nature and where the tidy pattern of fields emphasises the grander sweep of the hills. At one moment can be seen Exmoor's Dunkery Beacon, 29 miles away on Exmoor, and the sea fifteen miles away between Sidmouth and Budleigh Salterton, so clearly visible from the terrace of Wolford Lodge. The Wellington Monument draws the eye before letting it fall into the valleys below. There is a sense of immense space and freedom and the sky and its everchanging clouds stretch far away, transforming the land into patches of sun and shade under breeze and gale or closing in with driving rain or enveloping mist. Other corners of the Parish contain almost claustrophobic lanes, narrow and high-hedged, with only the odd glimpse of tantalising views. The changing seasons work their own magic, too. In Spring, the suddenness of the arrival of a mantle of translucent, shimmering yellow-green, particularly along the ancient hedgerows, takes away the breath; the dark brown of Winter is eclipsed, there is the promise of growth and renewal, especially in the clear stripes of the newly cut hay fields, and a sense of delicacy before the lushness of Summer. Very rarely does the area lose its green as the showers freshen the growth nurtured by the earlier rains. Autumn, too, is sudden; the Summer green is capped by the colours of fire before the leaves fall and the beech trees and hedges glow in their shades of old gold, to bring cheer and dignity to the white austerity of Winter.

The Blackdown Hills are not really hills in the accepted sense but consist of a high plateau, which falls steeply on the northern edges and dips away more gently in the south, with its water carved valleys. There is a marked contrast between the flat upland area and the more sheltered, richer and more farmed valleys. In Dunkeswell Parish, there is a surface layer of clay, containing flints and chert (a form of silica which may have begun as a jellylike ooze modified in time by hydration and the deposition of silica from marine sponge fragments). This is a poor, slightly acidic soil. Under it is the Upper Greensand deposit of some 30 metres thickness, formed in the Cretaceous period, a hundred million years ago, consisting of unconsolidated, fine-grained sands, again with flints, chert and siliceous sandstones and many well preserved fossils. Called Greensand, it is more often brownish in colour, particularly where stained by limonite or bog iron ore, though it has green patches. Grave digging in the churchyards in the Parish reveals the green, which has been caused by the mineral glauconite and which is known as Foxmould. Below the Greensand is a layer of Red Clays and mudstone, some two hundred and thirty million years old; where the Greensand and the Clay meet is the springline as the water cannot get through the impermeable substrata. From the springs have come the rivers of the area, especially the Madford River, flowing north and through by the Abbey to join the River Culm at Hemyock. There have also been landslips, as at Hutshayes Farm, and waterlogging at the junction of the strata. Geologists have shown that the whole area was a shallow, quietwater sea, about 200 fathoms/360 metres deep. It still surprises that shell fossils are turned up in gardens well up in the Hills; some of the best ones are just over the Parish boundary, at Blackborough, where the whetstone miners found fossil selling a profitable sideline. About 1800, General Simcoe took the French geologist, de Luc, round the Parish and to Blackborough, to show him how good and varied the fossils were. The whole area is displayed most graphically in the nineteenth century one inch Ordnance Survey maps, the relevant sheet for Dunkeswell being No.83 (Tiverton and Taunton); the dark hachuring sets off the plateau and the valleys very clearly.

The weather is all important to a farming community; the vagaries of the climate bring a patient acceptance by the farmers who have a strong belief that nature will work for good, that a long drought will, in the end, be relieved by a sufficiency of rain, and how right they are. The knowledge that Dunkeswell was invariably a few degrees colder and a few inches wetter than other parts of Devon, because it is some 800 feet/

240 metres above sea level, is borne out by the figures of the Meteorological Station established on the airfield in 1992, but Dunkeswell can be a place of sun and warmth and clear air. The Simcoe family commended the Wolford climate as being favourable and in 1794 the Rev.John Swete, the inveterate traveller round Devon, found Wolford a balmy spot after the Blackdowns in general, that "region of want and hills and stoney roads". A letter to the Simcoes in Canada, two years before, had complained of the great heat; "We are as scorched in England at the same time as at Niagara." That a change of climate was beneficial at times is shown by the Simcoes' purchase of Simcoe House in Budleigh Salterton, the small resort fast attracting visitors in the early nineteenth century, to which the family could go, for two or three months in the summer, for the fashionable and healthy seaside atmosphere.

Despite the beautiful Springs and long, hot Summers, it must always be the extremes that stay in the memory, although records are either of fairly recent date, part of the general climate of Devon and England or incidental to records of sickness; in 1540, Devon had a great drought, which produced the "sickly Summer" in which water shortages caused cattle to die and drinking water to run low and be contaminated, leading to dysentry or "the Bloody Flux". In 1739, there was the "Hellish Winter" which began on 24th December and went through the next eight weeks with severe frost when "cattle in the stalls died of cold, the trees split asunder and crows and other birds fell to the ground, frozen in their flight". A sudden thaw and rain on 1st January only made matters worse when frost reasserted itself and the "nasty Itch" was prevalent amongst those who washed infrequently in the bitter weather. 1814 opened with severe weather and 1855 saw another hard start to the year, as did 1881 and 1891, when there was a severe blizzard. One winter between 1816 and 1840 was bad and John Bailey, the Simcoe coachman, noted it in his journal. Mrs.Elizabeth Posthuma Simcoe was a great stickler for the attendance of family and Wolford estate employees at church and John Bailey wrote how deep snow, level with the hedges, never stopped Mrs.Simcoe and her household getting to Church and how she expected the Vicar to be there for every service. Earlier, in 1793, guests at Wolford Lodge had had to remain an extra three days in March because the snow had made the roads impassible.

Dunkeswell School and Dunkeswell Abbey School records are full of weather details. It is probably a myth perpetuated by us and our ancestors that "nothing stopped us from getting to school !". The records show otherwise and that was a matter of concern to the two schools as poor attendance meant less grant aid and the Mistresses were often asking that certain weeks' attendance figures should be discounted on the grounds of poor weather; the 1895 HMI inspection of the Abbey School commented that bad weather had seriously affected the progress of the pupils, especially as "some of the children have to walk so far to get to their homes", as the Mistress was to note in 1902. Poor little Minnie Clapp had to walk from Stentwood to the Abbey, at the age of four; the Mistress and the Clapps agreed on 28th February, 1894, that Minnie should stay at home until the better weather because "it is a bad path for so young a child in the Winter". The Abbey School in 1891 was closed for 13 days because of heavy snow and 2 days for heavy rain; the entry for 10th March read, "The School closed in consequence of the roads being so blocked with snow that the children were unable to come." Dunkeswell School in 1929 shut for 10 days because of snow and 2 days because of heavy rain. When the weather was not severe enough for the schools to close officially, there were still comments about the climate and the keepers of the log books either praised those few children who arrived at school, noted sadly the numbers of those who did not or simply recorded the weather - at the Abbey School, "a very wet, rough day" (1895), "the inclemency of the weather" (1900), "the rain simply coming down in torrents" (1903),"terrible rain" (1908), "abnormally wet" (1922 & 1923), and at Dunkeswell School, "a terrific thunderstorm from 8.45 to 9.30 a.m."(1918), "Miss Pratt was unable to reach school today because of heavy snow" (1941), "the playground strewn with ice covered branches" (1947). For the Abbey School, flooding was a great nuisance in the comparatively low lying area. On 12th December, 1893, no children arrived "on account of the weather and the rapid rising of the waters", the School shut for two days in the November of 1894, few attended in the middle week of December, 1897, and so the record went on. "The waters are out over the fields" in February, 1904; one boy fell into the deep water on 19th October, 1908, and parents had to carry their children home after school was over, so rapid had been the flooding; children arrived with soaked boots on 22nd February, 1910, and water was nearly over the footbridge; on 8th May,

1913, the Vicar closed the School because all the bridges were under water and the boys brave enough to wade through were very wet; the water was too deep for anyone to arrive on 9th March, 1914, and the "school offices were one foot under water"; ironically, even the Attendance Officer had to wade the river when the bridges were again under water on 17th February, 1915; and Arnold Doble was sent home on 8th August, 1917, when he managed to fall into the swollen river. Icy roads also caused absenteeism on several occasions and the room used as a school for the evacuee children in Dunkeswell in 1940 proved too cold for teaching for two weeks in February and the evacuees joined the Dunkeswell children in their schoolroom. No scholar reached Dunkeswell School on 2nd February, 1947, because of a blizzard which shut the School for several days; when it did reopen, no meals were able to get through from Honiton. More severe weather closed in during March, when "the playground was strewn with ice covered branches".

Other records show further hard winters. W.I. recollections show that, in 1944, the snow was high as the hedges and the tractors simply drove over them and a "Wrangle" occurred in 1947, when heavy frost and ice simply flattened the hedges and branches broke off trees. In 1962, the last week in December ushered in a long period of cold weather, with icy East winds; a slight thaw at the end of January was quickly replaced by more frost and snow lay on the ground for seven weeks, until the temperature rose dramatically on 3rd March. At the end of January, 1963, PC David Ware had to report "on extraneous duties performed due to exceptional weather conditions during January". The Parish Magazine noted that bricks, heated overnight in the oven, had to be placed at the feet of the Church organist in 1971 and the villagers complained strongly about the length of time they were cut off by snow in March, 1978. Percy Hill has always been hazardous for traffic in cold weather. Even today, newcomers are warned by the old hands, with a certain relish, to get in enough food and fuel to last for several days; recent winters have been much milder, although 1993 saw a white Christmas. Being cut off by snow has usually generated a great community spirit in Dunkeswell and a recollection of its former self-sufficiency.

Chapter 3

Settlements

Early man left traces of settlement in the two Round Barrows on the southern edge of the Parish, constructed in the Bronze Age, between 2,000 and 550 BC. They were fairly large, saucer Barrows but the growth of vegetation, farming and, probably, some basic excavation have all helped to blur their outlines and lessen their size. More misshaping occurred as late as 1940, when Local Defence Volunteers dug in to ready made firing ranges, unconsciously imitating their C14th ancestors who had practised week after week with their longbows at the butts. Men, women and children of the Iron Age, the Dumnonii, may have wandered through the area, along recognised trackways to Hembury Fort and elsewhere, which crossed in the Wolford area of the Parish but they left no records of their activities.

In 55 AD, the Second Roman Legion ignored the Blackdown Hills on its march to Isca Dumnoniorum (Exeter), although it established a temporary settlement at nearby Hembury Fort. The Romans stayed in Isca Dumnoniorum for three centuries and their extension of the Fosse Way led through Honiton and the valleys; they had still not penetrated the Blackdowns when they marched away early in the fifth century. Eventually, the Romans and the Britons were replaced by the Saxons, although the Saxon invasion of Devon was a prolonged business and a piecemeal conquest. As the Saxons occupied more of East Devon, they either enslaved the native population or drove it into exile westwards or across the Channel, to Brittany, or, more probably, they absorbed the Celtic people by marriage and the common ties of agriculture and trade. One Saxon tribe or family in the eighth century decided to settle where the church now stands as its leader recognised the many advantages of the site.

Dunkeswell is a good example of the natural instincts displayed by the original settlers in choosing sites, when they had no heavy and specialised equipment for creating an artificial settlement and were not dependent on any road system or the demands of transport. They and the land fitted snugly together; had they not done so, communities could not have grown. Centuries later, another settlement occurred and that, too, took advantage of the area but with modern technology, central planning and less natural instinct; there was a need for housing in the East Devon countryside and there was a large area of rather blighted land, much lying derelict after the American occupation in the Second War and given over to a scrap business. That scrap business had led to a string of complaints from the Parish Council, through the 1960s, with requests that it should be screened or removed, certainly the roadside dumps. To the potential builders and the planners it appeared that the chance had come to develop an area within easy reach of Honiton and with an already established community. To local people, the prospect of a well established estate seemed preferable to a wasteland. So, some years after the original plans of 1972, they built an estate on the hill top very much exposed to the cold winds off the Blackdown plateau and the mists, brought in all the main services except gas and created what became an estate very detached from the original village. Plans for easy road and pavement connections between the two parts were abandoned. Cyril and Hilda Cligg, who owned and worked Percy Farm, were surprised to learn that the 1970 planners had earmarked part of their land, at the top of Percy Hill, for a school, but that plan was also dropped; the chance to amalgamate new and old inhabitants through a common interest in their children's education was thrown away and the children ferried daily away from home into Honiton and Broadhembury.

The Saxons were wiser; experienced eyes looked and saw that the place was good. There was a water supply from the springs from the hillside, especially in the present Springfield area by the Royal Oak and Spring Cottage by the Post Office, and wells could be dug when needed; indeed, the water supply was so plentiful and pure that the Parish Council as late as August, 1935, under the Chairmanship of E.J.Baker, decided that the Honiton Rural District Council scheme for mains water should be rejected as a new Parish Pump had just been installed at Wellsteps. It was the building of the airfield in the 1940s and the coming of the United States Navy that finally brought piped water to Dunkeswell. The sloping site ensured good drainage of the Upper Greensand into the Madford Brook and that stream was ideal for the later building of a mill. The Saxons must have stood where the Chapel now is and realised how much shelter the hill afforded; looking across the village from the same spot, now, the fact that the top of the church tower appears slightly below the viewer shows how much protection there is from two sides. Building materials were readily to hand, with plenty of timber and an easily dug supply of chert with which so many houses have been built. Fuel was at hand, not only wood but also turf. There was plenty of land and agriculture could be carried on, even if at little more than subsistence level. The remoteness of the site and the potential for defence against human intruders were also important. So, in the eighth century, roots were put down.

By 1086, when the Domesday Book was made, the settlement had flourished and its importance been recognised by both Saxon and Norman Kings. In that year, William the Conqueror wanted to know exactly what he owned and how much should be paid to his Exchequer in feudal dues and taxes so the manor of Dunkeswell was visited by the King's Commissioners. With monks as clerks and soldiers as protectors and rounders up of the possibly hostile and certainly bewildered villagers, a thorough survey of Dunkeswell was made. It was determined who owned the land and how much it had been worth in the time of King Edward the Confessor, who had died in 1066 and been replaced by the unfortunate Harold; William treated Harold as an usurper and ignored his brief reign. Then, by determined questioning and an inspection, the Commissioners learnt how much the land was worth and how much could be paid to the King. It was a neat, quickly executed piece of work. The results went to Exeter and were transcribed into Liber Exoniensis, the Exeter Book; from there, the edited material was taken to Winchester and put in the national survey, the whole Book being produced in a very short space of time. The actual entry for Dunkeswell read:

Ipse.Ra.ten(tenet) DODUCESWILLA. Almer teneb.(tenebat) T.R.E.] geldb,(geldabat) p.(pro) una hida] (et) dimid. Tra.e.x.car.(carucas)m In dmio.e. 1 car.] III ferui] XI.uitti cu.(cum) V.car.Ibi.IIII.ac.pti.(prati) VIII ac.filuae minutiae.] X.q.pasturae.Olim] modo.val.L.solid

That looks pretty formidable to read, mainly because of the monks' shorthand and the Latin, but it translates fairly easily. The extra details from the Exeter Book appear in brackets:

Ralph holds Dunkeswell himself. Aelmer held it before 1066. It paid tax for 1½ hides. Land for 10 ploughs. In Lordship 1 plough; 3 slaves

(½ a hide) 11 villagers with 5 ploughs (and 1 hide and 1 virgate). Meadow, 4 acres; underwood, 8 acres; pasture, 10 furlongs (6 cattle, 10 goats, 50 sheep.) Value formerly and now 50 shillings

So, Dunkeswell was a small village but one well worth holding. It had belonged to Aelmer the Saxon, T.R.E. - in the time of King Edward - then was given by the King to Ralph de Pomeroi(Pomeroy), who held many other manors in Devon; Sir Ralph was rewarded for his faith in his Duke, whom he had followed from Normandy. Those listed were the heads of households so the population would have been about sixty. It may be strange to us to see that there were actual slaves listed but they were quite common and the conditions of some of the feudal serfs were little better than those of the slaves. The value of the manor had stayed steady from 1066 to 1086, being taxed for 1½ hides, a hide being about 120 acres. The Lord of the Manor had his own parcel of land or demesne, the ½ hide mentioned, and there he farmed with the labour of the villagers for so many days or hours a week and with special help at seedtime and harvest.

Dunkeswell not only was worth while possessing but it was also a flourishing manor; it did not decline into a mere hamlet, as some 60% of settlements listed in Domesday Book did. It had more history than 40 other Devon Parishes, which had no entry in 1086. Financial stringency or a lack of interest in a rather remote manor led to Dunkeswell being mortgaged to one Amadio, a Jew, for 80 marks, before it was redeemed by William, Lord Brewer, before 1200. This was the man who was high in the regard of Richard I, created Dunkeswell Abbey and put Dunkeswell on the map of thirteenth century England. The Abbey grew proportionally more important than the original settlement and that became known as "Old Dunkeswell" in deeds and agreements about land tenure, as in the leasing of "a tenement called Tenserye and some other parcels of land in Olde Dunkeswell" in September, 1533, and of "the corn mill of Olde Dunkeswell with appurtenances" in September, 1538.

The history of Dunkeswell changed from the time of the building of the Abbey; it was no longer a self-contained manor but very much under the power of the Abbot and linked with other properties given to the Abbey. When the Abbey was dissolved, in 1539, Dunkeswell reverted to the Crown, passing through a series of lords of the manor until the time of the Simcoes, whose control of the village lasted until the great Wolford Estate sale of 1923. After that, the village came more and more part of the system of local government, under Parish Council, Rural District and District Councils and the County Council; it still looked for a lead from Wolford Lodge but had a great deal more independence than before.

Apart from the main village, there were other settlements in Dunkeswell; the Abbey was the most important and that will be dealt with in another chapter. There was a small nucleus of habitation round Knapp, the sloping hillside, with a farm, a carpenter's and wheelwright's shop, a sawpit, a blacksmith and a public house there in the nineteenth century and small, worked fields round them, connected by footpaths to the main village. Devon Directories record the names of some who lived there; James Cox is listed as the blacksmith in 1870 and in 1879/80, and James Clode was the wheelwright in 1889. One path from the settlement led up to Hutshayes Farm and, in the lane just below the farm, were two cottages, the front wall bases of which can still be seen in the hedge and their gardens on the other side of the lane. The cottages rejoiced in the delightful name of Precious Court, although they must have been small and spartan and were empty by 1900.

Perhaps the most fascinating settlement was the one at Stentwood, for it was the creation of a Victorian "Squire", John Alfred Joseph Eccles. In 1881/2 he built a large house for himself, with a bailiff's house and a coachman's house beside it, in the lee of the hill. One of the outbuildings was a large conservatory in which vines and other fruit trees grew and the sheltered garden was a delight. Further up the hill, he built Home Farm, along model lines. For the house, he used stone and there was brick for the other buildings and the farm. In essence, it was a unit dominated by the owner and run on strict lines, as when all the farmhands and servants gathered daily in the small chapel which is still part of the bailiff's house; after prayers, the duties for the day were allocated. In its day, the estate must have been part Victorian and part medieval, the latest machinery running with the class structure of earlier times. Now, there is little to hint at past splendour; time and neglect have robbed it of its vitality, the splendid iron gates on to the Hemyock road have gone and the empty farmhouse no longer directs the work on the surrounding fields.

There are smaller settlements within the Parish, such as the large, outlying farms, some built after the enclosure and consolidation of agricultural land. In all, Dunkeswell is a widespread series of units but the core still lies within Old Dunkeswell, even with the expansion of the large estate at Highfield.

Chapter 4

St.Petroc and St.Nicholas

It was missionaries from Cornwall who brought Christianity to Dunkeswell, in the name of St.Petroc, and it was the old, Celtic form of Christianity that they brought. St.Petroc greatly admired accounts of the work of St.Patrick in Ireland, which ended with his death in 461. Patrick had sent his followers across to Scotland and down to Wales and the West Country; Petroc himself may have heard the word of God in Wales or in Cornwall and he, as a Bishop, sent out missionaries before his own death in 594. In all probability, Petroc himself never came to Dunkeswell and we do not know whether his priests came before the Saxon settlement or after. If after, it is likely that the Saxon and pagan customs prevailed for a while; if before, then the missionaries would have erected a crude shelter, probably close to where the Church stands now, inaugurating a period of nearly twelve hundred years of Christian worship.

In time, the stronger, Roman form of Christianity prevailed in Dunkeswell; the English Church, begun by St.Augustine in 597, was a well organised one, with support from the Continent and the beginnings of wealth that enabled churches and monasteries to be created. There was a spur, too, from the Norman regime in England, when many of the Bishops in England were Normans and tightly linked with Rome. The decay of Celtic Christianity may have brought about the confusion over Dunkeswell's patron saint, with Patrick apparently replacing Petroc, so that medieval revels were held round the Well of St.Petroc and in the Churchyard on St.Patrick's Day, 17th March. It was probably easier for the people to associate their Church with a Saint who had a special day of the year, one of the many Holy Days which brought the poor a general relief from the drudgery of their daily lives and routine.

Some form of permanent building was erected and that was replaced by a grander church after the founding of Dunkeswell Abbey; the Abbey inspired and financed the new church and, to ease the Saintly confusion, named it after St.Nicholas. On 5th December, 1259, "in Vigilia sei Nich.", the Bishop of Exeter, Walter Bronescombe, dedicated the

Church to the genial Patron Saint of children. A mythology had grown up around the figure of that Bishop in the Roman Empire, who had suffered imprisonment and torture at the hands of the Romans and been resilient enough to win his release and spend fruitful years before he died in 326. The two most famous stories about him recount how his generosity enabled three young girls to have wedding dowries in purses thrown down the chimney and how he restored to life three young boys who had been killed, cut up and pickled by an unscrupulous innkeeper, ready to make pie fillings. He was a proper saint for the pre-Christmas period!

The Tithes of Dunkeswell had been given to the Abbey and, in return, the Abbey financed and staffed the church and took it under its wing. In 1261, for example, Bishop Bronescombe ordered the Abbot to pay a stipend of 5½ marks a year to the Vicar, with special legacies, corn dues and offerings at the greater Festivals of the Church. Religious life in Dunkeswell was, therefore, closely bound up with the Abbey and it felt the reverberations of both the Dissolution of the Abbey in 1539 and the violent Prayer Book Rebellion of 1549, before settling down as part of the reformed Church of England. There had been mention of Thomas, "Parson of Donkeswille" in 1119, then long gaps until 1740, after which time the list of Vicars, Rectors and Perpetual Curates is almost complete to the present day. That the incumbent was appointed by the Abbey ensured that any gap in office could be covered by the monks; loss of Parish records meant that later Ministers were unknown except when their names cropped up in state records, such as the Devon Protestation Return of 1641. The Protestation, "to protect the true reformed Protestant religion expressed in the doctrine of the Church of England, against all Popery .... for the defence of His Majesty's royal Person, Honour and Estate, as also the Powers and Privileges of Parliament, the Lawful Rights and Liberties of the Subject"; in other words, the Long Parliament was testing the waters in the days of rising protests against Charles I and his Archbishop, William Laud, recently imprisoned in the Tower of London. Of the 86 names of men over 18 on the Dunkeswell list, 82 were in the same hand, presumably because they were illiterate. Four only signed their own names; the High Constable and Warden with the romantic name of Honyball Rawe was one, although he appears in other documents as the more prosaic Hannibal, the Petty Constable Andrew Whithorn, the Overseer of the Poor Theophilus Marwood and the Minister himself, Prosper Blayney. In 1674, the Clayhidon Rector, who was also Rural Dean of the Dunkeswell Deanery, complained to the Bishop of Exeter that there was "no minister who officiates either at Sheldon or Dunxwell" and stated one Thomas, who was "bound to pay a certain stipend yearly", very seldom had anyone officiating and "I suppose the stipend is for the greater part put up in his own purse", a sad but common enough state of affairs. Earlier, Dunkeswell must have been weakened for there are complaints about disputes over seating in the church; Peter Bartoes, of Awliscombe but having estates in Dunkeswell, could not get seats for himself and his family in 1663 while, two years later, Peter Barlowe had special seats for his family which destroyed the uniformity of the seating and blocked the way to the bell tower. Later reports by the Rural Dean complain of repairs being needed to seats and fabric and a lack of surplices in 1740, with the tower "out of repair". Milles Parochial Returns of 1755 described Dunkeswell Church as having one "isle", with a slate and lead roof, and a West tower with a 30 foot high wooden steeple on it. In the same year, the Rev. Nicholas Lockyer was without paten or flagon, although the records show there had been a large pewter flagon, a silver basin and a silver plate in 1725 and that the present silver chalice, silver paten and silver alms bowl had been made in Exeter by William Pierce and hallmarked in 1754; perhaps they were brought from elsewhere in response to the complaint. The same Nicholas Lockyer had had to lay down the law to his parishioners for their neglect of the churchyard and remind them that they had to maintain the bounds in good repair; he had also had to remind his flock that the Clerk and the Sexton both had to be paid by the Churchwardens. The actual Church had to be maintained by the parishioners while the Chancel was kept in good order by the Impropriator or collector of Tithes. It was not always easy to get money out of the hands of the Impropriator, especially when Nicholas Lockyer, being Perpetual Curate, actually had no house in the parish.

Tithes had been in the hands of the Abbey until they passed to lay owners or Impropriators in 1539, who virtually fixed the salary of the incumbent, who figures as a Perpetual Curate, the lowest order of three, a Vicar or a Rector. It was possible, therefore, to have a wealthy "living" but a poor incumbent without even a house in the Parish; in theory, it would have been possible for a Roman Catholic to have taken the Tithes, as happened in other places. A Vicar was one who was put in a "vicarious" position, that is, was put in to do the duty of another, the Impropriator; the Thesaurus Ecclesiasticus of 1782 and 1788 record that the Rev.William Jenkins was Vicar and that he had been appointed by Peter Genest to a parish of £16 yearly value. A Rector was one who had Tithes paid directly to him. The present incumbent is both a Rector (of Dunkeswell) and a Vicar (of Sheldon), hence he insists that his place of residence is called the Wreckage!

When the Rev.John Clarke came to Dunkeswell in 1814, the year when the long war against the French first ended and Napoleon was exiled to Elba, he found a mixed state of affairs. He had no house in the Parish and lived in the Rectory at Clayhidon, his other benefice. The thirteenth century church was "in a very ruinous and decayed state"; at the same time, it was too small for the congregation he had. In response to the questions of the Bishop of Exeter in 1821, John Clarke recorded that there were 81 families in the Dunkeswell Parish and, of those, some forty or fifty came to the Sacrament of the Lord's Supper, which service he held four times a year. Other services were held throughout the year but never more than one on a Sunday; that service began at 1.30 p.m. and contained a sermon. That service was the one that had always been held, as stated, "during the Memory of Men". There was the service of the Sacrament of the Lord's Supper, which attracted forty to fifty communicants; that service started earlier than 1.30. There was no regular Catechism of Youth although there was a Sunday School supported by public subscription. Being a man of action, John Clarke approached his Churchwarden, Joseph Manley, and a special Vestry Meeting in October, 1816, agreed that the cracked and dangerous North and South walls should be demolished and rebuilt, the lead on the roof should be sold for funds and all the roof slated, the gallery should be rebuilt, the main seating removed and refixed, the broken floor repaired and new North and South Aisles constructed. The pews continued to be allocated to families but it was ensured that certain pews should be retained for the poor of the Parish. Work began in 1817 and was completed in the same year; it is impossible to know what was actually left of the original building. Perhaps the luck of the horseshoe fixed on the door in 1828, its ten nails representing the ten churches of the Dunkeswell Deanery, ran out; by 1848, the church was described as "being in bad style". The Rural Dean commented on its condition in his visitations over several years; the roof needed repair in 1826, the walls were damp inside and the Children's gallery needed a railing for its stone steps. Three years later, he made adverse comments about the chancel roof and, in 1836, noted main roof repairs were needed and the walls were damp again. On all occasions, whitewashing was needed. Our Churchwardens can but feel for their predecessors.

Neglect spread outside the church; in 1831, the Rural Dean complained that "the Churchyard is often stocked with horses", although he did manage to get a wall built round the churchyard in 1838, presumably to keep out horses and stock. In that year, he reminded the Churchwardens to change "King" to "Queen" in the Altar and Prayer Books, after the accession to the throne of the young Victoria. He had to speak to the Churchwardens again in 1850, about the shortcomings of the Sexton and "his great neglect of duty in allowing nettles and weeds to overrun the churchyard" and he requested "the Churchwardens that (the Sexton's) duties for the future may be more satisfactorily performed". The Church had to accommodate over two hundred people each week at alternate Morning and Evening services, according to the Religious Census of 1851; the average attendance for 1850/1851 was 160 adults and 48 Sunday School children each Sunday, some of whom went to the other service at the Abbey.

With the evident faults of the Church building in front of them, the parishioners were not altogether surprised that there had to be another rebuilding, between 1865 and 1868; Services were conducted in the Schoolroom and in Wolford Chapel, which was licensed to allow the seven marriages and nine baptisms to be conducted there. C.F.Edwards was the architect of the new church and he designed it in "a handsome Early English style", with room for two hundred "seatings"; again, it is not recorded if any part of the older church buildings was incorporated into the new one. The Simcoe family came to the rescue, once more, and the interest and generosity of the six Simcoe sisters (Eliza, Charlotte, Henrietta Maria, Caroline, Sophie Jemima and Katharine) are recorded on the flag draped tablet inside the main door and their faces look down from the corbels in the nave on the church they helped to build. The sisters were carved and identified by their initials by Henry Ezard, the commission being his last work before he died in 1868, as recorded in the North Aisle. Richard Croly, the incumbent, gave much personal attention to the work and his daughter was responsible for the illuminated lettering on zinc of the Ten Commandments, the Creed and the Lord's Prayer contained within the blind arcade of the reredos. He was aided by the Churchwardens over the three years, Robert Smith, Joseph Burrows and William Clements.

A special, large pew was made and reserved for the use of the Simcoes; the view from it now is obstructed by the pulpit but, before that was resited, the Wolford Lodge party could have a clear view of both clergy and people, especially the Wolford Estate workers, who were expected to attend Church every Sunday and who were rebuked when they failed to be there; bad weather was no excuse for absence. John Bailey, the Simcoes' footman from 1816 and coachman from 1836, wrote, "I have known when the snow had been up level with the hedges and no horse or carriage able to go, the ladies and servants all set off, the men in front one after another to tread down the snow, then the ladies and the maidservants in our tracks. We had no reason to think that the deepness of the snow would prevent Mr.Clarke from coming to church, as I never remember him, not once, for the cause of bad weather to miss coming." Another witness to the effect a later Mrs.Simcoe was to have was Peggy Primrose Farmer, who was born in 1900 and was the mother of Ann, Ivor and Malcolm Stevens, all still resident in the village. She made some notes on her early days and, even though brought up on a non-Simcoe owned farm, Connetts, recalled that Mrs.Simcoe used to arrive at Church in a carriage and pair, with a footman to open and close her carriage door; "if we were driving to Church in our trap and if we saw the Wolford carriage already in the village, Mother would whip the pony and hurry him on, afraid of being late. The Church was full every Sunday and Mrs.Simcoe would see that all her servants were there and all her tenants, their wives and families, and you had to have a reasonable excuse if you wanted to stay away. I remember two pews full of her indoor servants. She used to provide their hats or, rather, black bonnets tied with black ribbon. I thought they were nuns for years." John Bailey said that the Wolford Lodge contingent very often occupied at least half the seats in the Church.

In 1868, the Rural Dean congratulated "the Parishioners on the erection of a Church worthy of the House of God"; the Vestry meeting was even more effusive and it recorded "deep gratitude and thankfulness that the Parish Church has been rebuilt in a manner so worthy of the House of God and that the fact of the Fabric not only being rebuilt but the interior fitted up for their accommodation, without any expense at their (the Vestry's) hands" and the meeting "strongly called upon the Vestry to complete their Church by rebuilding the Tower". The money for the Tower was to be £280, to be borrowed "upon the credit of the Church Rates", with interest not to exceed 5% and to be repaid in seven equal and annual instalments; the following year, the Church Rate was bumped up from ½d. in the £ to 1d. and Charles T.Edward, of Exeter, was commissioned as architect and Joseph Rockell, Stretchley Churchill and James Turner as builders. The rise in the Church Rate led to some opposition, the Vestry minutes in 1869 agreeing "by the majority of the Ratepayers present that the Churchwardens do take such legal steps for the recovery of the Rate as they shall be advised by their lawyer". Samuel Marks and William Clements, Churchwardens, must have found that an embarrassing task; they could not have been entirely successful as the Rate soared to 4d. in the £ in 1875, to complete the repayment of the Tower loan.

St Nicholas's Church

Richard Croly left in 1874; his successors to St.Nicholas's and Holy Trinity at the Abbey congratulated themselves on having two new churches but William Balmain and Henry Selby-Hele were both faced by disturbing reports. The Rural Dean reported in 1878 in Dunkeswell that "the Church is in a very unsatisfactory state; the wet penetrates the walls on all sides and the water plates are crumbling away". That was a mere ten years after the church had been built. Selby-Hele in 1879 was informed that "the Church is in a worse condition than last year; the water tables are in a state of complete decay". A "thorough repair" was effected in 1881; in 1884, however, the walls were wet and again in 1886, when the coping stones were found to be decayed and the tower pointing bad. The gate pillars were rebuilt in 1894. In 1896, the Rural Dean got to the root of the problem; "the inferior stone used at the Restoration of the Body of the Church has led to many defects through frost." After substantial repairs and stone replacement in 1898, the Rural Dean was able to report that things were better and the Church was being kept in excellent order.

Not only was it inferior stone used but an inspection of the tower in 1947 revealed that it was in such a dangerous state that the bells should cease being rung immediately, then taken down and the tower itself demolished. Mr.Prewett, of Harbottle, Reed and Ham of Exeter, saw that the weight of the flat roof and the bells had caused the upper part of the walls to break free of their corners, there was a lack of bonding of the random stones and flint with poor mortar in the building and the structure was weak through a shoddy rubble and mortar core. The whole trouble had been aggravated by the strong vibrations of the heavy engines of the Liberators and Catalinas on the wartime airfield. The Parochial Church Council had to act swiftly, securing special bell lowering equipment and estimates for a new tower. For the following few years, there existed a strange situation. How was the PCC to raise £800 to pull down the tower and another £3000 to rebuild it ? As its appeal to the US Embassy stated, "this is a very tiny and poor parish", with only 380 people and two churches and two chapels. With great faith, the tower was pulled down and the West end of the Church covered with sheets of corrugated iron while the Parish set to work to raise money. It was agreed that there should be no commercialism, although appeals were made to wealthy Americans, such as Joseph P.Kennedy, USN veterans, the BBC and the Martyrs' Memorial and C of E Trust. For much of his Rectorship, 19471954, Robert Vokes was concerned about finance. In the end, after further frost damage in the winter of 1952/3, work went ahead and the new tower, lower and less pinnacled than the old, was consecrated by the Bishop of Crediton in July, 1954, leaving the Parish with a debt to be paid and the bells to be rehung. The bells had stood on the floor of the church and were examined by the Whitechapel Bell Foundry in 1955; a long pause ensued. Then, fund raising, especially by the Carnival Committee, came to the rescue, a Faculty was granted and, in December, 1959, on the 700th anniversary of the 1259 church, the Dean of Exeter dedicated the five refurbished bells and the one new bell, the Treble which bore the names of the Rector, W.F.Williams, and the Churchwardens, W.F. & H.J.Farmer.

From all the rebuilding, the notable survival was that of the octagonal Norman font, the best part of the furnishings. Carved in about 1200, it is rather crude in construction and repair but, below its plaited girdle, there are two rows of scallop ornamentation and, above, columns containing figures and these figures are most interesting. They may not be entirely clear, either in outline or symbolism, and many have pondered on their meaning. In the centre, facing east, is a bishop, robed in his chasuble and holding a pastoral staff; then, from left to right, are a man and a woman, the prow of a boat or a beaked head, a scaly elephant, an archer shooting an arrow at the elephant panel, a man holding a crosshandled sword, a crowned king with a sword and shield and, finally, a man in chains. Interpretations have been many and varied. Could the bishop have been St.Nicholas ? Perhaps, but the dedication of the Church to him came later. Were the man and woman Lord and Lady Brewer, to commemorate their endowment of the Abbey in 1201 ? Was the boat the Ark or connected with St.Nicholas ? Was the archer shooting at dangers confronting Christians ? Did the man with the sword and the crowned king represent temporal power ? Was the chained figure that of St.Peter ad vincula (in chains) ? Most fascinating is the elephant, evoked from early descriptions of the fabulous beast; it is recorded that the first elephant to be brought to England was in 1255 and the font representation may well have been one of the earliest in this country. The Roman author, Pliny, had described the scales on an elephant and how it used them to crush flies which settled on it, an unlikely piece of biological engineering. The elephant also had the reputation of giving birth in water, so deterring any dragons which might devour the calf; there may be a dragon seen below the elephant on the font. If so, then the symbolism is one of Baptism, a new birth through water. It is a fascinating thought that Baptisms have been held in the font for nearly eight hundred years, giving a deep sense of the influence of the church in village life.

Another survivor is the Vicary tablet behind the organ, recording four members of the family between 1561 and 1604. Other memorials are connected with the Simcoe family, Elizabeth Charlesworth and her lengthening of the Nave "for the Poor of Dunkeswell", the two Great Wars and the US Navy and the east window, which glows in the morning sunshine and emphasises the concept of the Resurrection through the sowing and reaping of corn and the long service given to the parish by the Farmer family.

The bells provide a challenge for any tower builder when a peal is being rung, with great stresses and strains. The six bells are mounted on ball bearings in a cast iron frame and they are rung regularly. Two of the bells (4th & 5th) bear the name Thomas Davy, 1684, and another (Tenor) the name of the Church Warden of 1732, William Denner, with Thomas Wroth added. To mark the 1865-68 building, Captain J.K.Simcoe, R.N., of Wolford Lodge, presented one more bell (2nd) and the Rate Payers of Dunkeswell another (3rd) in 1870. The final bell (Treble) came in 1959.

The ministry in Dunkeswell was very much in the hands of a powerful family or organisation until this century. The Abbey held the right to fill the living until 1539, then it passed to the Crown. In 1614, it is recorded that the Rectory and Church of "Old Dunkeswell" went to Francis Morrice and Francis Phillips, for services to James I, who had put the living into the Duchy of Lancaster. Later still, James II, between 1685 and 1688, granted the living to Anthony Crewe and William Stucky. In 1743, the Patron of the living was Peter Genest and he paid the Licensed Curate £16 a year; then and later there had been augmentations or increases in stipends from the C of E source, Queen Anne's Bounty, with some land being bought in Hemyock "for the Benefit of the Curates of Dunkeswell for ever". Peter Genest's daughter, Sophia, took on his rights before they went to Sir Thomas Graves who passed it to his daughter.

Through the Simcoe/Graves connection, the Patronage came into the Simcoe family and, after the General's death in 1806, his widow became Patron. Affected deeply by the death of her husband and living on until 1850, Elizabeth Posthuma Simcoe found solace in the management of the Wolford Estate and, with her many daughters, in the Church and good works; she has been described as "the moral squire" of Dunkeswell. Each day at Wolford Lodge began with family prayers in the parlour. Mrs.Simcoe had been caught up in the Evangelical Movement of the early nineteenth century, especially when she stayed in London, and approved its influence against the dreaded anarchy of the post-1815 period and such an event as the 1819 Peterloo Massacre in Manchester. Agrarian unrest of the time might have spread to Dunkeswell and the Movement was a positive influence through its policies of building more churches, giving more education and being strictly Sabbatarian. Mrs.Simcoe found the simplicity of St.Nicholas's "so Protestantlike" and added a plain gallery to the Church in 1832. She appreciated good sermons. The Curate, James Temple Mansel, preached an admired sermon in 1839 but it was deemed "not energetic enough for the poor", of whose welfare and moral behaviour she was always conscious. In that respect, the later Mrs.Mary Simcoe, who died in 1920, followed her precepts; girls connected with the Estate were given copies of the Bible nine months after their marriage but only if they had by then produced no children, while pregnant but unmarried mothers who lived in Wolford estate houses were expelled from their cottages. If they did not go, then the whole family was evicted. Elizabeth and her daughters shared the spiritual work of the Parish, especially in charities and church building; they also supported neighbouring projects, as in Elizabeth's generous donation to the Hemyock Church restoration of 1846 and her daughters' contribution to the church in Canada in 1854. Eliza Simcoe had a special interest in the Abbey, Anne in Dunkeswell and Caroline in Luppitt. The Patronage passed to John Kennaway Simcoe, then to Arthur Henry (Linton) Simcoe, who, in 1923 put into the Estate sale not only "a singularly delightful residential site" and a "glorious panorama of the well wooded and boldly undulating country" but the Lordship of the Manor of Dunkeswell and "the advowson and rights and nomination and presentation to the Perpetual Curacy of the Parish Church of Dunkeswell". That was purchased by Basil Oliver who, in turn, sold to

Alfred Le Marchant. Eventually, the Patronage went to The Martyrs' Memorial and C of E Trust, which now appoints the Rector of Dunkeswell. The situation became complicated in 1972, when the Rector took on Sheldon Parish as well, as Vicar; the appointment of Vicar lay with the Bishop of Exeter, and there was a dispute about appointments. The following year, the Church Commissioners decided that the Martyrs' Memorial would appoint the next two incumbents, the Bishop the third.

From 1842 to 1874, John Clarke, Theodore Muller - an unusual appointment of a German-born Rector to Dunkeswell - and Richard Croly had all been responsible for Elizabeth Simcoe's Church of the Holy Trinity at the Abbey and that church returned to the Dunkeswell Rectors in 1929. Richard Croly and his family had lived in Blackdown Cottage, in the centre of the village, until the Rectory was built in the late 1860s.

The Exeter Diocese appointed the Rev.Stuart Worth, Rector of Dunkeswell, to be Priest-in-charge of Luppitt, a Parish which looked more towards Upottery and Monkton than across Luppitt Common to Dunkeswell. The grand idea was to have a Team Ministry for Dunkeswell, the Abbey, Sheldon, Luppitt, Upottery and Monkton, with a Rector at Dunkeswell and an appointment made for Team Vicar at Luppitt. However, more Diocesan decisions were made, the new Team Rector from London declined the post of Priest-in-charge of Luppitt and the Dunkeswell/Luppitt union ceased, to be taken up again by the Rev.Nicholas Wall after 1978, thus giving him the responsibility for four churches, the fast growing Highfield Estate, a busy schedule and the building of a new Rectory in Dunkeswell.

Chapter 5

Church and Chapel

There are and have been other non-Anglican places of worship within the present Parish. Presbyterianism had become strong in England during the Civil War but, after Charles II returned, the Church of England's supporters tried to ensure that the supremacy of their Church was not challenged again. In 1665, the Five Mile Act was passed as part of a series of Acts against Dissenters; it forbade any clergyman or teacher to come within five miles of a city or corporate town unless he swore "that he would not at any time attempt any alteration in Government either in Church or State". Hence, the recorded existence of a Presbyterian community in Dunkeswell between 1672 and 1690 may have been due to its convenient distance from the Borough of Honiton; it left no written records behind, mainly because it would have depended on the Church of England for matters such as marriage and burial and because any records were the property of the Minister rather than the church. The Act also accounts for the Magistrates in Quarter Sessions in 1707 notifying and recording "that the house of John Griffin in Dunkeswell is appointed and used for a place of Religious Worship". Again, no records to show what sort of Dissenting church it was.

Dissenters were not rigorously pursued by the law in the West Country and Methodism spread widely after 1740, when John Wesley broke from the Established Church; many of the 200,000 miles he travelled in preaching missions were in Devon and Cornwall. Methodists attracted followers by their clear and popular Christian message and others joined who may have resented the injustices, class rigidity and parochialism of the Church of England. The Dunkeswell Replies to the Bishop's Survey of 1821 show that there were two families of dissenters within the Parish but that many who worshipped in St.Nicholas's also went to Prayer Meetings, perhaps for more inspirational religion. Early in the nineteenth century, Methodists from Branscombe formed a congregation in Dunkeswell. Mr.Huniball, or Honniball, and others walked from Branscombe on Sundays and back

The Methodist Chapel

again and held meetings in John Rowe's Cottage, later Rose Cottage and now Millbrook, by Dunkeswell Mill; this was a building licensed by the Magistrates for Public Meeting.

In 1849, the Taunton Congregation built the Chapel in Dunkeswell, the date and TC being carved on a beam, and it quickly flourished. In the Religious Census of 1851, Samuel Farrant, "local Preacher of Dunkeswell" from Connetts Farm, was able to report that there were 35 Free Sittings and 70 other Sittings for worshippers and that the attendance on 30th March had been 51 in the morning and 54 in the afternoon; the year's averages had been 50 and 70. The popularity of the afternoon service at the Chapel remained until 1993, when it was decided to change to a morning service, except on occasions such as Harvest Festival.

For family reasons, the Chapel was part of the Taunton Circuit; then, it was directed from Wellington, with preachers driving over for morning and evening worship, leaving the trap in the shed and the horse in the field. Preachers also came from Honiton. If a preacher could not reach Dunkeswell, then one of John Wesley's or George Whitefield's sermons would be read, although some members of the congregation found those overlong. Some preachers, such as the Farrants, lived or stayed in the village. Dunkeswell Chapel was famed for its missionary services, when as many as three missionaries might be seated on the platform.

Music was important and there was a fine choir, supported by wind and string instruments until the purchase of an harmonium, bought and played by Frank Rowe, later by the Misses Farrant. The Chapel had its

Wolford Chapel

own burial ground, although early Methodist burials had been legally enforced within the Church of England and the Parish Records contain details of Methodist burials. Now, there is a Steward in the village and a strong fellowship with St.Nicholas's.

The present Wolford Chapel was mainly the work of General Simcoe and was built in 1801/2, although it incorporates some of the groundwork and walling of the original chapel dedicated to Wulfere/ Wulphere, the King of Mercia from 657 to 675; he had been the first King of Mercia to convert to Christianity and his daughter, Werburgh, became an Abbess. In the rivalry between the Anglo-Saxon kingdoms, the Mercians had swept down from the Midlands, had become overlords of the West Saxons in the eighth century, and had tried to secure the border with the original British in Devon. The Dunkeswell Saxons could have come with the army or in its wake. At the edges of the Mercian conquests in Wessex, several chapels were built; there was the Wolford one, with others at the two Woolfardisworthys (near Crediton and Hartland) and at Membury, St.Werburgh's. Wulferchirche may have been so called from the Old English Wulffordcirice, the Church by the wolf fold, but it is the King's name still commemorated on

Highfield. The Chapel had been granted to Dunkeswell Abbey by King John about 1200 and gradually decayed after the Dissolution of the Monasteries.

General Simcoe wished to have a family chapel, for devotional and personal reasons, and he and Elizabeth oversaw the construction of the small, plain building. It was not an entirely new building but rested on the foundations and lower walls of the old Chapel, parts of which can still be seen; as such, it was an already consecrated site. There were new furnishings and others which came from older churches; the panelling on the North Wall is reputed to have been taken from St.Nicholas's, at a time when it was in a ruinous state, and parts of the altar panelling, reading desk, seats and some bench ends came from elsewhere. There are three funeral hatchments on the walls, bearing Simcoe and Gwillim arms, the latter being Elizabeth's family. The first great ceremony in the Chapel was the 1806 torchlit funeral of Simcoe himself and there are memorial stones to him, his wife and five of their children at the base of the eastern and southern external walls; it was found that the coffin plate and the memorial to the General differed as to his exact age. During the 1865/8 rebuilding of St.Nicholas's, the Bishop granted special dispensation for services of the Parish Church to take place at Wolford, as noted in the Church records, as well as in the Dunkeswell Parish Room.

In itself, the Chapel is an interesting building, with a splendid view to the sea, but it strongly serves as an Anglo-Canadian memorial to the work of Simcoe as Lieutenant-Governor of the Province of Upper Canada, 1791 - 1796. The new Province, originally based on Newark or Niagara-on-the-Lake and later at the new capital of Toronto, owed much to the General's dedicated service, in which he had the support of his wife, Elizabeth Posthuma Simcoe. The 1965 John Graves Simcoe Memorial Foundation undertook the restoration of the Chapel and the deeds and property were handed over to the Prime Minister of Ontario, John P.Robarts, in 1966 by Sir Geoffrey Harmsworth; Alfred Le Marchant, of Wolford Lodge, ensured that free access would always be available by donating right of way to the Chapel. Many Canadian visitors are attracted to Wolford and Canadian government policy stated that "it is appropriate to mark, maintain and foster the final resting place of John Graves Simcoe to the end that all who visit it will learn of his life and work for the Province of Ontario".

The Simcoe connection is also prominent and acknowledged in the Church of the Holy Trinity, at Dunkeswell Abbey, which is built on the site of the former Cistercian Abbey and incorporates some of the stonework from it. The family had always been interested in the Abbey ruins and had made various sketches of them, with reconstructions of the Abbey as it had been. Elizabeth Posthuma Simcoe was dismayed by the general neglect of both the area and the spiritual welfare of the Abbey inhabitants and she and her daughters set about raising money to build a church there. The Appeal letter stated that "anxiety for the restitution of what their forefathers once enjoyed has stirred up in the hearts of some a desire to build on this once consecrated spot a small and simple Church". The intention was to bring religious comfort to the three hundred living in the surrounding area, including Hemyock and Clayhidon, and to ease "the spiritual destitution" and the organisers appealed for subscriptions to be paid into the Bank of Messrs Flood & Lott, Honiton. It was hoped that local farmers would draw materials to the spot. The money did come in, fully supported by the Simcoe generosity, and £817 was spent on the building and furnishing of "The Church of the Holy Trinity, Dunkeswell".

Elizabeth endowed the Church, which she had conveyed to Her Majesty's Commissioners for building new churches, with a yearly Rent Charge from certain buildings and lands. These included the cottage and garden within the old Abbey ruins and "several closes of land" - the Croft, Churchyard Meadow, Bolton's Meadow, Ritchell's Ground, Abbey Close, Abbey Meadow (also called The Ham), Five Acres, Lower Kitchen Close, Higher Kitchen Close, Daws and Troakes Orchard. Away from the Abbey were the lands at Pit Place (known as Fancy) - Stover Close, Four Acres, Six Acres, Eight Acres, Gould Close, Great Slade, Lower Slade, Little Gould Close, Home Meadow, Orchard, Coppice, Twenty Acres, Little Close and Three Acres. With what little might come in as pew rents (1851, "only two families pay for sittings"), the money was to go towards the stipend of the officiating minister and the maintenance of the Church, its furnishings and churchyard. Katharine Simcoe gave Consolidated Bank Annuities for when the Church had its own incumbent and to build a suitable parsonage house at Henland, in the Parish of Hemyock; the house should be similar in style and size to Black Down Cottage, Dunkeswell, with a footbridge over the river, a garden for the incumbent, in one acre of ground and with four acres of pasture. The Vicarage was built in 1876, when a new ecclesiastical Parish was carved out of Dunkeswell, Hemyock and Clayhidon. Another Charity was set up, in 1859, in memory of Lieutenant Colonel John Lewis Black, who left £105 in his will, to be invested so that the interest should "provide a fund for the sustenation of the fabric" of the Church.

Much of the artistic planning of the Church and its windows, carvings and furniture was done at Wolford Lodge, where the Simcoe sisters had a long room in which they both designed and carved wood and stone. Many of their original designs are still in existence; some were colour washed, others were strongly drawn in very black ink with red and gold details. They were, in some cases, drawn on the backs of old letters, a bank receipt, the cover of an exercise book, an 1838 letter from Sidmouth, a Dinner acceptance and a laundry list; one of the window sketches had a sad note on the back - "You will not hear from the Wilsons. Poor Mr.W quite dying, probably all over by this time." - while another had part of an early Penny Red on its reverse. The sisters were very meticulous and it is interesting to compare their drawings with what is in the Church. They had sketches of work in other churches, there were carefully executed inscriptions, as for the font ("Suffer little children to come unto me and forbid them not."), the mailed arm from the family coat of arms, a series of snowflakes and leaves, even the roof pinnacle and turret, and a very detailed drawing of the reredos.

Holy Trinity Church

On 21st September, St.Matthew's Day, 1842, the Church was consecrated and served the Abbey people faithfully, with the large congregations recorded in the 1851 census. The morning congregation on 30th March had been 67 strong, with 31 children in the Sunday School, and the census had reckoned the yearly average to be a rather surprising 160 adults, with 32 children. Holy Trinity had its own Vicar from 1876 until 1929, when the Rev.Victor Edwin Seagrove had been there for twenty years and the Abbey passed back to the Rev.Charles Fookes, at Dunkeswell. The scheme "for effecting the union of the Benefice (being a Vicarage) of Dunkeswell and the Benefice (being a Vicarage) of Dunkeswell Abbey, Holy Trinity" had been proposed by the Bishop of Exeter to the Ecclesiastical Commissioners for England, approved "by His Majesty in Council" and promulgated in "The London Gazette", 13th August, 1926. The anniversary of the consecration was celebrated every St.Matthew's Day and a whole day's holiday given to the Abbey School pupils; the 50th anniversary, in 1892, warranted two days off school. Every year, there was a lavish spread laid on for the children's tea in the schoolroom, where one of the Simcoe family presided. Sometimes, the children were taken for their tea to Wolford Lodge. Now, the few regular services held there are supplemented by ones for special occasions, reminders of the days when the Church was a centre and the hard, very upright pews were filled. The sun shines through the Simcoe glass and the singing rises into the loftiness of the roof. The Church is of a very simple and rather cold, bare and puritanical design but with constant echoes of the love and dedication that went into its original foundation.

Now a Listed Building, Grade II, it was built on the site of the old Abbey church of local stone, much of it from the old ruins, flint rubble and hamstone dressings and detail, with a slate roof, surmounted by an apex cross at the East end and a polygonal, stone bellcote at the West. The Church is long and tall, with a narrow South aisle and a porch and vestry at the West end. The main floor is tiled and there are some of the original Abbey tiles in the Sanctuary. The reredos is like the one in St.Nicholas's, a Beerstone blind arcade, inscribed with the Lord's Prayer and the Ten Commandments, and there is a Beerstone font, with a large, octagonal bowl. The Church stands in its own churchyard and is approached along a leafy path; it is very much in the fields which so occupied the minds and strength of its original congregation and amongst the ruins of the Abbey which inspired its building.

The Abbey Baptist Chapel, showing the exposed rectangle of original wall.

A surprising omission from local directories and Exeter records and reference books is the Baptist Chapel at the Abbey. The Baptist sect had been started in Amsterdam in 1609 by John Smyth, an English religious refugee; it believed in Baptism for believers only and that by total immersion. Over the years, the Baptists had split between the General and the Particular, the New and the Old Connections, until the 1813 Baptist Union called for closer co-operation. Baptists had been active in the Abbey area in the nineteenth

Musgrove Farm

century and they were determined to have their own Chapel, instead of going to Hemyock.

The Baptist Church annual report for 1906 recorded that the new Chapel had been opened at the Abbey, "where cottage meetings had been held for twenty years". A suitable site had been given by F.Smith, of Pitt Farm, Willand; William Doble presented the necessary building stone, which was carried to the site by volunteer hauliers and worked on by volunteer labourers, as many as thirteen at a time, under R.Hill. Edward Lutley, of Hemyock, was the volunteer architect and supervisor of the works. The actual cost went above the estimated £150, to £199.4.4, but the annual report stated that it "opened free of debt". There was £19 short on opening day and that money was found by the hat going twice round the assembled guests.

Opening Day was 12th October, 1905, when the Abbey School Mistress reported that attendance for the school day had been poor because "the children at the opening of the new Chapel". A large crowd, from as far afield as Minehead, was present to hear the new Pastor, Thomas Brain, conduct a service of prayer, hymns and addresses; many had to stand throughout, such was the press in the Chapel. After the service, there was a tea for nearly 200 people in a freshly decorated barn at Musgrove Farm and then an evening meeting for some 300 people, in which six more addresses were given. Trusteees were appointed, on the understanding that if there were under 12 regular communicants for a period of six months or low attendance for a year, the Chapel and the Musgrove Farm field added to it in 1916 would go back into the hands of the Trustees, for them to dispose of according to law. The Chapel had an active life as a virtual mission station, with Sunday School on Saturdays and Sundays and an afternoon service for all on Sundays. It came under the supervision of Hemyock and was linked with Sainthill and Bolham Water. Chapel and Church worked closely together; often, the afternoon congregation at the Chapel proceeded en masse to Evensong at Holy Trinity. Alfred Oliver Doble, of Madford Farm, was Deacon and Sunday School Superintendent of the Chapel for many years. The last appointment of Trustees took place in March, 1945; they were Alfred Wide, William John Ayres, The Devon Baptists Associated Corporation Ltd., William Oatway Turner, Howard Laurence Wide, Alfred Oliver Doble, Sidney Stevens, Ronald Alfred Doble, Gordon James Farmer Stevens and Clifford John William Doble.

The last service in the Chapel was on 9th October, 1966, and the Chapel reverted to the Trustees, who sold it by public auction in Hemyock on 16th August, 1968. In 1972, G.Pring, the Hemyock builder, was given permission to convert the Chapel into a private dwelling, "Abbey Chapel"; he enlarged the building but left exposed on the end wall a large rectangle of the original stonework, as a reminder of its past

Such is the width of the Christian religion that it accommodated yet another influence within the Parish and that was the Blackdowns Mission, although the nearest Chapel was close to Sheldon Church. The Mission was the idea of the 7th Day Adventists at Clayhidon and it was put into practice by George Brealey, in 1863. He shared Mrs.Simcoe's views on the spiritual neglect of the area but perhaps he did not fully understand the people with whom he was dealing when he wrote, "The major part of the people (of the Blackdowns) could neither read nor write ...... in some of these districts there existed as gross ignorance and superstition as are to be found in many heathen lands." The Rev.Mr.Swete had been equally gloomy in his travels at the end of the eighteenth century and he also had undervalued the true worth of the local people.

Chapter 6

The Cistercian Abbey

The Cistercians came to build their Abbey at Dunkeswell in 1201. That, in itself, was significant in the history of the monastic movement and it had widespread consequences for the small Manor in which the Abbey grew. Dunkeswell was opened to many influences; it became part of the national and international sphere of the monks, was brought closer to the King and his Council and came under the sway of two of the most powerful royal ministers of their time, playing its part in the general pattern of the rise and fall of the monasteries.

By the end of the eleventh century, many of the ideals of the early monks, such as the powerful Benedictine Order, had been submerged in growing wealth and temporal power and there was a wish to restore simplicity of worship and life. In 1098, a group of reforming Benedictines founded an Abbey in Burgundy, at Citeaux, the Latin form of which was Cistercium. One of its monks became the voice and inspiration of the reformers; between 1113 and his death in 1153, St.Bernard of Clairvaux led the Cistercians to create some 340 houses all over Europe as men responded eagerly to his leadership. They were not only the monks but also rich and successful men of the world who gave land and financial support to the growing movement.

The creation of Dunkeswell Abbey followed the strict rules for the location of a new religious house. There had to be at least twelve monks for a new foundation, which should be built in an isolated spot, "far from the concourse of men"; the buildings had to be plain and simple, without any ostentatious ornament. The monks themselves were to work with their hands, to restore the forgotten dignity of labour, as well as worship God in a routine of strict rules of silence and diet. They were to wear the undyed, woollen robes, which gave them their name of the White Monks, and wool was to be the basis of their finances.

On 15th August, 1201, there was a special meeting of the Convent (the coming together) of Forde Abbey; the assembled monks were headed by their Abbot and the Abbot of their Mother house, Waverley.

The laity was powerfully represented by Lord William Brewer. The Convent chose the necessary twelve monks to build the new Abbey at Dunkeswell and added Gregory, a lay workman with the skill to direct the construction. There was time for some hutted accommodation to be built for them before they actually arrived on site, on 16th November.

The site was excellent. "The Gentleman's Magazine", of 1791, described it as being "in a picturesque valley, whose richness confirms the general observation of the monks choosing spots of the highest fertility for their residences. This valley, terminated by surrounding hills, extends every way about two miles, excepting on the South side, which is open." It was isolated enough for Cistercian rules, it was good for agriculture, there was plenty of swiftly flowing water for domestic, fishing and milling purposes, Collards and Abbey Hills sheltered it from the winds that blow over the Blackdowns, and it was close enough to both Dunkeswell village and Lord Brewer's hunting lodge and kennels to have a ready labour supply and contact with the lay founder. The lodge was reputed to have been Brewershayes, from which name came Bowerhayes; however, the Burehege or Bureheye of 1206 had an Old English derivation, the hedge/enclosure at the burh/settlement, of which Bowerhayes was a later corruption.

The Abbey could never have been built unless spiritual devotion had been supported by temporal riches and there was, at hand, a wealthy and powerful patron, Lord Brewer. He had been born about 1150 and took an interest in Dunkeswell when he redeemed land that had been mortgaged to Amadio, a Jew. He became Sheriff of Devon from 1179 to 1189 and a judge under Henry II and Richard I. When Richard left England for the Crusades, in 1190, the realm was governed by a committee of the judiciary; the Bishop of Durham and William de Mandeville led and William Brewer was one of four judges with them. The judges' power lessened when William de Longchamps took over and combined the offices of Justiciar, Chancellor and Legate but Lord Brewer was powerful enough to be prominent in the ransoming of his King, who had been captured by Leopold, Duke of Austria, in December, 1192, on his way home from the Holy Land. He was active in the securing of Richard's freedom, taking money and 67 hostages to the Holy Roman Emperor, one of the hostages being his own son, William. Richard came home in 1194 and the hostages followed. Lord Brewer continued to serve both Richard and John and his eminence was confirmed by his signature on Magna Carta in 1215. He had been Sheriff of Cornwall in 1202 and 1203 and then Sheriff of Dorset and Somerset in 1209; he was overzealous in taking taxes and the men of the two counties complained about him in 1210 and refused to have him as Sheriff again. He was the only Sheriff who signed Magna Carta and kept his office, as Sheriff of Hampshire, and he was considered one of the crueller and more oppressive administrators under both Richard and John.

It may not have been surprising, therefore, that, in the Charter for the foundation of Dunkeswell Abbey, Lord Brewer prayed not only for "the salvation of the souls of my Lords Henry and Richard, Kings of England" but also for the salvation of "the souls of my father and mother, and my soul and those of Beatrice, my wife, and my children..." or that, later, he found the burden of authority too great for him to bear. His wife, Beatrice de Vallibus, had died in 1217, his son, William, had grown strong, his daughter Alice had married Sir Reginald de Mohun (from which alliance was descended the Simcoe family) and he, himself, was feeling his age. Thus, in 1224, he renounced all his wordly wealth, asking the young Henry III to accept the homage of his son, William, for his lands, and became a lay brother in Dunkeswell Abbey, on the terms that he should be buried before the Great Altar of the Lady Chapel, alongside his wife. The monks honoured their promise in 1226. Later, in the hot and parching summer of 1852, a workman discovered two stone coffins in an indentation in the Abbey land; the remains of a man and a woman were put together in one of the coffins and reburied, the second coffin marking the burial place before it was brought into the new church.

Giraldus Cambrensis, in his autobiography of 1179, dealt with monasticism; "It is ordained by the Cistercians 'That in future neither farms nor pastures shall be purchased and that they shall be satisfied with those alone which have been freely and unconditionally bestowed upon them.'" To begin with, the Abbey abided by the regulation and accepted gifts of land from many donors; all was given to the Abbey with the direct or indirect intention that the monks should pray for the souls of the donors, as in the case of Lord Brewer in 1201 and in 1224, when he gave the Manor of Lincumbe (Ilfracombe) for the burning of a candle "for the salvation of his soul". In 1255, the Abbot agreed to accept Peter and Alienora le Bon "into all the benefits and orisons which hereafter shall be done in his Church for ever", for land in Ruffgreihays; the next year, he did the same for John and Nichola de Gendeford, for land in Hembury.

Lord Brewer's original grant of land was generous, being "all my lands in Donkewell and Wulferchurch with the advowson of the churches of the aforesaid lands"; between 1206 and 1217, he added the 620 acres of Hembury Manor and the Manors of Collaton (Raleigh) and Uffculme, with its mill. Gifts from others were confirmed by a Charter of 1206 from King John; they included Bywood (from the Abbot of Forde and Lord Brewer's son, Ursus), 30 acres near Bowerhayes (Richard of Hidon), Bantesnappe (Dunkeswell - from Richard of Treminetes and William of Pinu), 8 acres at Stentwood (John of Treiton), the 167 acre Manor of Sobbecombe (Luppitt - from Yvonis, son of Allan), land at Marlcombe (Awliscombe - from Richard of Manelega), 8 acres in Uggaton (Philip of Gatiden) and lands in Lynor (Hackpen - from Robert, son of Amicia of Dunkeswell, and Ursus Brewer). Gifts came in fairly regularly; Amicia of Dunkeswell herself gave Hoked in 1227 and William Brewer the younger left his estate at Buckland Brewer in his will in 1233. Land within the Parish was 80 acres at Ruffgreihays in 1253 and more there in. The tenements in Exeter and Honiton were gifts, probably for town houses for the Abbot. The one in Exeter was in the Parish of St.Paul, convenient for the Abbot to conduct diocesan business with the Bishop; the one in the High Street in Honiton, perhaps the present Manor House by the Baptist Chapel, he would have used for conducting the affairs of his Gittisham estate. is only later that the Abbey actually bought land and became engaged in land and tithe controversies, as at Doddeton in 1259 and Upottery in 1291. By the end, the Abbey had about 10,000 acres of land. In 1291, for the taxation of Pope Nicholas IV, the value of its Manor of Wulferchurche was £5.80, Biwode £3.30, Burhei and Steintewode £4.30, Dunkeswell £2.20 and its Church £5.00. After acquiring Dunkeswell and Wolford Churches in 1201, the Abbey added the Churches at Dotton (Collaton Raleigh) in 1242 and Sheldon and Awliscombe in 1243. Much of the Abbot's time was taken with the administrative and legal aspects of the large estate.

Naturally, the chief concern of the Abbot was to run a godly house, within the terms of the Cistercian Order, and his house would be autonomous. However, he had to submit to an annual inspection by the

Abbot of Forde, just as the Abbot of Forde was inspected annually by the Abbot of Waverley. The Abbot of Forde was certainly at Dunkeswell in 1508 when an alleged attack upon the Abbey took place and he was able to corroborate the Dunkeswell testimony. Every three years, there was a visit by inspectors from Citeaux and, every year, the Abbot had to go to Citeaux, for the General Chapter of the Cistercian Order, leaving the Prior in charge at home. It must have been a considerable journey via Dover but it was always undertaken, usually under the protection of the King (1285 - "Protection for the Abbot of Donkeswell going beyond the seas") but also if it meant defiance of the King, for one reason or another. It is known that the Abbot, on his return from the General Chapter of 1308, was actually arrested by the Constable of Dover for failing to have the King's Licence to go overseas; the Constable of 1334 was requested to assist the Abbot go to France although he had not obtained (i.e.bought) a royal Licence. Because of its system of rigorous inspection, the Cistercian Order was a popular one in England. Dunkeswell had no Bishop's Visitations and there seem to have been few complaints about Dunkeswell before the Dissolution.

The Abbot also had to attend the General Convocation of the Clergy in St.Paul's, each year, where he was influential in deciding policy on matters such as support for Crusades, ecclesiastical taxation and the definition of heresy and action against it. On occasions, he was summoned to London for other reasons. In 1235, he had to answer before the King's Bench for failure to pay the dues on the Manors of Lincumbe and Buckland Brewer; he had gone to plead his case before Henry III at Winchester, to no avail, and the King's Bench made him pay the dues. In 1240, it was the turn of the Papal Legate to call the Abbot to London; that was a more successful visit as he and the other Abbots refused to raise money for the Pope's war against the Holy Roman Emperor, Frederick, even though the King supported the Legate. In 1441, the Abbot was again called to London, to answer for Dunkeswell's non-payment of Papal dues.

Money was always difficult. When lands were given to the Abbey, they were generally exempted from paying tithes; in the words of Lord Brewer's 1201 Charter, land was given "in free, pure and perpetual alms, quit of all services and secular exactions", but that was forgotten more and more, leading to court squabbles. In addition, Kings demanded money; Edward I's 1276 war against Llewellyn had to be paid for and the English Cistercians were asked for £1,000, with Dunkeswell producing nearly £15. In 1302, Edward I took the Abbey's money that should have gone to Citeaux. In 1332, Edward III demanded a subsidy on the occasion of his sister's marriage; John de Bruxton was sent from London to collect the money from Dunkeswell. In 1522, Henry VIII demanded the Abbey pay £100 annually for the recovery of the crown in France. It was always a struggle to pay, especially if the Treasurer of the Abbey was as inefficient as the one taken to court by the Abbot in 1326; William Vyncent had failed to produce the accounts of the Abbey and was ordered so to do.

At home, the Abbot had to co-ordinate the various activities and sections of the Abbey, religious and secular. Just as the monks had started their building work with the Church, with the eastern end and the Lady Chapel being built first and then the Nave end, so he had to balance the needs and duties of both the choir monks and the lay brothers, the conversi. He oversaw the conduct of worship, the eating and sleeping arrangements, the well ordered sanitary arrangements, the relief of the poor and the sick and the orphans, education of all within and some without the Abbey and the Abbey's connection with Rewley House and St.Bernard's College at Oxford, his manors and granges, agricultural and industrial techniques, public relations and good will. In the daily Chapter, he maintained discipline in his house or asked for outside help, as in 1346, when he asked that Brother John de Pernyle, "who has spurned the habit of his Order and is now a vagabond in secular attire", should be found and arrested, to face Abbey chastisement. In the end, the Abbot and his subordinates could no longer exist within the framework of the Cistercian life of simplicity. That was especially so after the disorganisation and lawlessness caused by the Black Death of 1348. Much of the work force was lost and agricultural depression followed, deepened by the creation of a wage-earning and mobile labouring class and a fall in the number of monks, down to only eight in 1377. Violence was used against the Abbot, monks and Abbey. Yet, it was the increase in violent vagrancy and disturbed rural areas that sent men to the shelter and the certainty of the Abbey. There were twenty monks there by 1400, although they may have had a less austere and deeply religious life than the early monks and were asked to do less of the physical labour that had been the Cistercian ideal.

By 1524, the Abbey was becoming apprehensive about the policies of Henry VIII and his ministers; in that year, some of the smaller monasteries were dissolved by Cardinal Wolsey. In 1529, on the pretext of the annulment of his marriage with Catherine of Aragon, Henry had summoned what became known as the Reformation Parliament, which saw through the breakaway from the Pope and the creation of Henry as Head of the Church in England. A logical consequence of that was the ending of any monastic ties outside England and the suppression of the allegedly wealthy monasteries, to finance the King's grandiose schemes. The King's Vicar General, Thomas Cromwell, sent round teams of Commissioners to assess the spiritual and temporal value of the monasteries. In Dunkeswell, the years 1533 to 1538 saw a flurry of requests for legal tenancy agreements, against the evil days to come. The last Abbot, John Ley (Lee) had to give a detailed evaluation of the Abbey in 1536; on Easter Day, he stated on oath that the Abbey's value was £294.2.9. That made Dunkeswell seventh in the table of larger monasteries in Devon; Plympton and Tavistock were the largest, valued at £912 and £902 respectively, with Newenham and Canonsleigh at the lower end, with £231 and £197.

After that, the Abbey could do nothing but wait. News of the surrender of the smaller monasteries came to Dunkeswell; the Abbot maintained the daily routine as best he could and found himself appointed Collector of the Clerical Subsidy for the King, although he was dilatory about his returns to the Bishop of Exeter. Then, the end was brutally simple. On 14th February, 1539, Commissioner John Tregonwell brought the Deed of Surrender. The Abbot assembled his monks, the deed was read to them and they were asked to sign; there can have been little hesitation for they knew they had no choice and their signatures on the document are firm and clear. Abbot John Ley signed first, then his nine brothers. John Tregonwell's men saw the monks off the premises, made a thorough search of the Abbey buildings and despatched precious items to London, so that the official report could be made to Thomas Cromwell, dated 20th February, from Exeter. Even at that stage, the Commissioners tried to justify the closure of Dunkeswell Abbey and the others; they wrote that there had been no trouble but that they had found "great waste and many leases lately passed which they have stayed and called in again".

The monks had had time to prepare themselves and plan for their future but they must have left the Abbey with a sense of loss. They all, except for William Roseter and John Hayward, are listed as having been awarded pensions. The Abbot received £50 a year and became Rector of Sheldon and Sainthill; later, he moved to Payhembury. Another monk, John Gaye, became Curate at Sheldon, with a pension of £6.13.4. For the rest, pensions ranged from Steward John Webbe's £6 to John Benette's £4.13.4. Technically, half yearly payments were made in London, but they were probably collected by an agent; his fees and those of the London officials would have reduced the pensions but none of the monks could have been badly off.

As for the Abbey itself and its great possessions, they came directly under Henry VIII. To reward faithful service, most went to John, 1st Baron Russell; as President of the King's Council in the Western Parts, he had almost vice-regal status and he was a man whom the King could trust implicitly. That trust was later vindicated, in 1549, when Edward VI's Council wanted decisive action in the Prayer Book Rebellion. With little delay, Henry granted him the Abbey building and site, land in Dunkeswell and Old Dunkeswell, the Abbey Granges of Bowerhayes, Bywood, Broadhembury and Sheldon, the Parish Church of Dunkeswell and the Church and Chapel at Awliscombe and the tithes and advowson on 1,600 acres, a total grant of some 6,000 acres. That was in addition to the gift of Tavistock Abbey; in all, Lord Russell took one sixth of all monastic land in the county, worth £1,050 a year. Remaining land of the Abbey was administered by the King's Council until most of it was sold off between 1543 and 1545 for £3,535, while the Manors of Wolveston and Broadhembury, valued at £1,220, were given as a gift to the Earl of Southampton, the King's Secretary. The King himself retained the Manor of Dunkeswell, the Abbey farm, Bowerhayes and Bywood Granges, a watermill, and some land in Luppitt, maintained by a Crown Bailiff at Bowerhayes. In time, this land passed from hand to hand until it became part of the Simcoe Estate.

The saddest part of the story was the ruin of the Abbey itself. Lord Russell had no interest in it, having stripped it of anything of value left behind by the Commissioners, including the four bells, some windows and glass and the lead from the roofs, and he sold the buildings to John Heydon, of Ottery St.Mary. He was to pull down and take away as much as he wanted within ten years from November, 1539, with the proviso that any treasure found should be shared with Lord Russell and that he should not benefit from anything found in tombs within the Church and Chancel. John Heydon worked thoroughly; what he did not take away, he burnt, leaving only a shell. The rood screen, separating nave and chancel, found its way to Feniton Church. After Heydon and his men left, some local people took what stone they wanted and others moved into the ruins, creating the squatters' "sheds" on which the Revd.John Swete was to comment later. It was a twilight world of lost buildings and lost ideals. The romanticism and sense of abandonment of the place affected visitors and General Simcoe and his family made many sketches of the Abbey ruins before Elizabeth Posthuma Simcoe and her daughters did their best to restore the religious atmosphere in their new Church of the Holy Trinity. Even today, the green tranquillity engenders that feeling of peace and quietness which so appealed to the Cistercians, nearly eight hundred years ago.

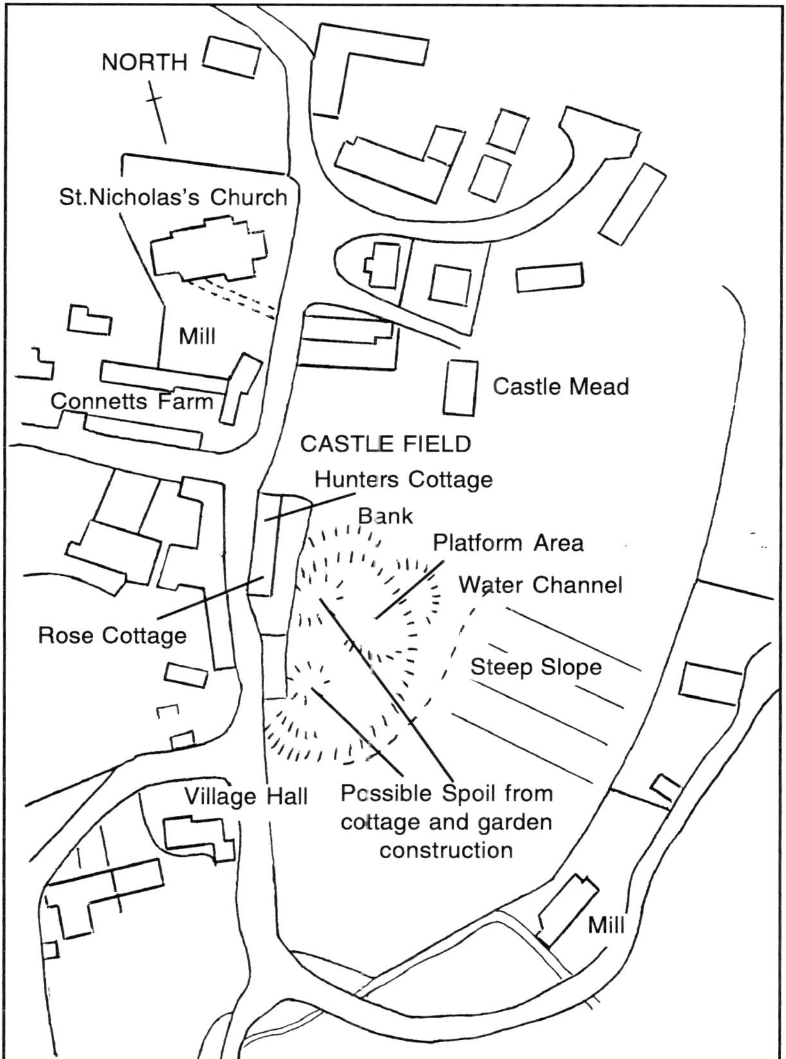

MAP 2: Dunkeswell Castle Site

Chapter 7

Wars and Rumours of Wars

Few settlements in England can claim to have been free of some military action in the course of their history but Dunkeswell was tucked away in the Blackdowns so that it avoided the Romans, gave little resistance to the Saxons, was too far from any Viking incursion and the Norman invasion of 1066 meant little more than a change of manor ownership. Peace hung over the village yet the tradition of there having been a castle in Dunkeswell has lingered on, apparently confirmed by the Tithe Survey map and schedule of 1841, where Fields No.69 & 70 are Castle Mead and Little Castle Mead, owned by Mrs.Elizabeth Simcoe and farmed by Robert Smith. Today, Castle Mead is the name of the bungalow that abuts Castle Field, part of Connetts Farm.

From the ground, little is visible of any castle but aerial photography clearly shows a small, oval enclosure on Castle Field and the 1:2500 O.S.map of 1984 marks the outlines of ramparts; there are two rows on the eastern side, short lines of a third rampart on the north and south and a small enclosure in the southeast corner, with Hunters and Rose Cottages and the road having obscured the western side. A castle on that site would have had a clear view over the sharp drop to the Madford Brook and would have been able to defend the village and church, with an ample water supply. On the other hand, there would have been the strong disadvantage of the site actually lying well below the higher ground above the church and capable of being dominated by superior forces. There seems to have been no documentary evidence of any castle, either in civil or ecclesiastical records, not even in the Abbey records, and any castle should have been of interest to a king and his financial advisers. Had there been a castle of any substance, then the building materials would have been reused, as those from the Abbey were, but there are no signs in village buildings of large, roughly dressed blocks of stone.

In 1975, Malcolm and Ann Stevens allowed the Devon Committee for Rescue Archaeology to excavate parts of Castle Field, before ploughing and reseeding took place. To begin with, the excavators thought they were looking at a late prehistoric settlement but a trench revealed a low bank of chert lumps and rough wall foundations and pieces of medieval pottery, from around 1250, including fragments of a jug imported from Normandy, corroded iron and three cow's teeth. Of 1,112 sherds excavated, only 74 were post-medieval. The archaeologists concluded that much pottery was coarseware but the fine white-cream jug indicated "that the occupants of the enclosure were above peasant status". So, it would appear that there was some ramparted strongpoint, perhaps a small compound for cattle and sheep, probably built in the thirteenth century, but one of uncertain use. It is not known if this small, roughly defended area was actually used or when it was allowed to fall into disuse. Suggestions were made that the area might have been one of the Abbey Granges, or outlying farms, which were occasionally surrounded by earthworks or moats; a Grange actually within a village was not usual, however. There might have been a hunting lodge connected with the monastic benefactor, William Brewer, or his heirs, although there is no documentary evidence for this.

Dunkeswell's participation in later troubles is also uncertain but events could hardly have passed by the village entirely. Henry VIII's destruction of the old religion in the Reformation was of much concern to Dunkeswell as it led to the Dissolution of the Abbey in 1539, an event which offended some and pleased others. Dunkeswell, with thoughts of spiritual and economic changes, would have observed events with interest. Yet the devoutly conservative nature of West Country men and women would have made them unprepared for the violence that was to erupt in 1549, under the young Edward VI. Henry VIII had defied the Pope, declared himself Head of the Church in England and had distributed Abbey lands; Edward's Protector, the Duke of Somerset, went further and faster and he and Edward and Archbishop Thomas Cranmer introduced a new and Protestant Prayer Book in English, to be the only legal form of worship in the English Church from Whitsun, 1549. Devon was a long way from the King's administrators in London and reacted slowly, hence the deadline suddenly became urgent and the proposed changes overwhelming; the old colour and rituals of generations would be lost and tradition violated. The outrage felt in Cornwall and Devon staggered the Court; the Protector urged conciliation, writing to the Devon gentry that the rebels had been led astray and could be pardoned. But rebellion swirled around East Devon and men from many villages went to join their protesting fellows. A king without any standing army would use troubleshooters and two of those were Sir Gawen Carew, in London, and his nephew, the Sir Peter Carew whose family lived at Mohun's Ottery, near Luppitt, were early Protestants and had interests in Dunkeswell. Sir Peter, who had gone to Exeter and St.Paul's Schools, had seen military service in France and was regarded as the local man to contain the Prayer Book Rebellion. He came down from Lincolnshire via London, and used speed, force and conciliation. The rebels were indignant when Carew's men burnt part of Crediton and they moved to besiege Exeter itself; Carew saw the threat and returned to London, to report personally to the Council. As a result, Somerset despatched Lord Russell and forces to Devon.

Russell was already known to Dunkeswell. Still President of the Council in the Western Parts and now Lord Privy Seal, he was a capable soldier with much land to defend in Devon. He had been told to take stern measures so "you shall be dread" and these orders would have gone to his agents in Dunkeswell; we do not know whether they cowed or inflamed the local men.

Russell and the Carews urged London to send more men; based in Honiton and Mohun's Ottery, they scoured the area for recruits but the few they found drifted away to the rebels at Exeter. So unusually depressed was Russell that he set off for Salisbury, only to be pulled back by the energetic Sir Peter.

In July, therefore, the rebels were in strength round Exeter, the royal forces lay in Honiton and both sides waited. Russell left Honiton, to burn part of Ottery St.Mary, and came back until news reached him that the rebels were determined to stake all on battle and had advanced to Fenny Bridges. It was there, in Blood Meadow, now Fennymead, just north of the present railway line and bridge, that fierce fighting occurred. The rebels refused to be tempted out from their strong position, inflicted many casualties with their longbows and, in the end, had to face a determined cavalry assault by Sir Peter and hand to hand fighting. In the end, of course, they broke and went back to Exeter, leaving their dead and wounded to the mercies of the royal mercenaries and their blood in the Otter. There was a last flicker of the rebel army at

Blood Meadow; 250 late arriving Cornishmen attacked and routed Russell's foot until they were overwhelmed by the regrouped royalists.

After that, Russell made a cautious advance on Exeter, raised the siege, took revenge on many rebels and seized more land before going back to London in late August, appointing a brutal Provost Marshall in his place. On his return in September, he sent ten ringleaders to London for trial; four of them were executed at Tyburn in the following January. In Devon itself, one of the measures that Russell imposed on all churches except those in Exeter was the silencing of the bells, even if simply by removing the clappers. This was from his fear that the bells would be "rung backwards", the term for ringing muffled bells to act as a tocsin to rouse the countryside; when he had advanced on Fenny Bridges, his men had been dismayed by the ringing of local bells, for a holy day, but Russell had feared they were a signal and did not forget.

Dunkeswell had to accept the silence and the Prayer Book and the reformed religion and, in the end, took the new liturgy to its heart so that it was ready to resist apparent advances to Rome in the following century.

Lord Russell continued to be familiar to Dunkeswell and he, as Lord Lieutenant of Devon, gave orders for the military Musters of the reign of Elizabeth I, when England was threatened by Spain. The Musters took place about every three years and were reviews of men and weapons; they were done at Parish level as the government was still fearful that mass gatherings of armed men might foment rebellion. The record of the 1569 Dunkeswell Muster still exists, with a list of "the names of all the habell men within the saide parishe mustered as biffore" and a report for the Deputy Lieutenants and the Sheriff. The three Presenters were John Phillip, Roger Jenynge and Nicholas Hurle who presented "as beffore said" all men between 16 and 60, as well as Winifred Buller, 21 in all. Winifred was a widow, as appears from a later document, with goods of her own, and she had to produce 1 Corslet (light body armour of breast and back plates), 1 Pike (15 foot long, singlespiked, iron bound against swords cuts and bill chops), 1 Harquebus (3 foot long early firearm, 10 lbs in weight, igniting gunpowder in a pan by a lighted wick, cumbersome and inaccurate) and 1 Murrion (ridged and narrow brimmed helmet). Winifred must have been relatively wealthy as others did not have to produce as much. There were no Parishioners in the richest Grade, the Light Horsemen, but several in Grade 7 (goods worth £10-£20) and 6 (£20-£40). Archers were men like John Phillip Junior and John Crowse; Richard Vycary and John Manley were Harquebusiers; Henry Ley and Thomas Ley carried Pikes, and Bills (6 foot agricultural bills with a spike) were paraded by the lowest group, men such as John Otterye and William Middleton.

Musters became of much greater importance as the Spanish menace grew larger. When the Armada set sail in 1588, the news of its arrival off the Lizard was carried quickly through the realm and to London. Beacons were manned day and night and the people of Dunkeswell would have heard the news when the beacons were lit; the village lay in the middle of five beacons - Blackborough, Dumpdon Hill and Beacon, Upottery, Culmstock and Ottery St.Mary. In all probability, the men of Dunkeswell looked out their weapons and stood to, as they were to do on future occasions.

Some of the weaponry recorded in the Muster Rolls may well have come out again in the Civil Wars of 1642-49, after a long period of peace. How the Wars affected Dunkeswell is tantalisingly unknown but there was military action in East Devon through the years and a campaign in each year from 1642 to 1646. The Cornish army went through Devon in 1642 and 1643, including its march from Tiverton via Cullompton and Honiton towards London. Charles I marched his army through Honiton, where he stayed on two occasions, to Exeter and Cornwall in 1644, and 1645 and 1646 saw the renowned New Model Army, under Lord Fairfax and Oliver Cromwell, passing through Honiton and Cullompton. There was also considerable activity in Taunton and some in Hemyock and its castle, held by Parliamentary forces in 1645.

The next agitation was caused by the Duke of Monmouth, bastard and Protestant son of Charles II, who had landed at Lyme Regis in 1685, to try to snatch the throne from his Roman Catholic uncle, James II. He made his way through Axminster to Chard and was crowned King at Taunton. En route, his Protestant rebels had raised men from the area of the march and the names of many of the rebels have been recorded and their subsequent fates after Monmouth's brave night march to defeat at Sedgemoor. Some were hanged, drawn and quartered, as in Honiton, and their quarters boiled and salted down and spread through the main towns of the county; others were sent as slaves to the West Indies and others were gaoled, fined or released. Many simply vanished. There are records of a large number of men from Honiton, two from Combe Raleigh, two from Sheldon, thirty four from Luppitt and thirty two from Upottery, large numbers for small villages. On Dunkeswell, silence, as there is on Hemyock, but it can be assumed that men went to fight for King Monmouth and were boosted by the prevailing optimism that Roman Catholicism would be driven out. What a sad disappointment they must have had, though they may have heard how God's vengeance brought lightning to strike John Boilman, the appropriately named man who had boiled the quarters in Taunton. Three years later, the Dunkeswell response to the landing of William of Orange in Torbay and and some of the Royal army declaring support for William in Honiton would have been careful.

The eighteenth century was a peaceful one but it ended with the new phenomenon of national warfare, with Britain and other European powers having to meet the might of the French Revolutionary armies and navy, from 1793 until the final defeat of Napoleon at Waterloo in 1815. For some of the time, Britain stood alone against France, until she could build up a new coalition, and the Royal Navy was her shield against invasion. Invasion was a very real threat and it was that fear that put Dunkeswell quite literally on the map. The government turned to two bodies, the Board of Ordnance (Gunnery) and Horse Guards (Army Staff), for surveys of the country, although they were rival and jealous organisations. The Board of Ordnance officers had developed a new theodolite and the triangulation system for mapping in 1791 and, in 1795, triangulation began in East Devon, although the numerous hills and trees made it hard so that the work had to be based on a line drawn at King's Sedgemoor, in Somerset. The War made it necessary for Ordnance to begin maps "marking ground for the encampment and exercise of Troops or for the purpose of superintending and directing the progress of Works for National Defence". Two years later, Horse Guards sent down to the West Country 700 regular cavalry and 5,00 regular infantry, to be supported by 2,000 militia horse and 17,000 militia foot, and they had a clearer idea of the layout of the land. In 1800, authority was given for the detailed mapping of Devon and most of the coast had been covered by 1803, mainly on a scale of 2 inches to the mile, with Dunkeswell appearing on Sheet 21 in October, 1805. All the Devon sheets appeared by 1809, although not on sale to the public, and there were several revisions of the work; the 6th Revision of 21 included the proposed Bristol/Exeter railway line, for example.

Dunkeswell was very much caught up in the invasion scares of 1803-5 which were ended by the naval victory at Trafalgar. So great was the relief at the destruction of the Franco-Spanish fleet that General Simcoe, of Wolford Lodge, ordered the guns of the Luppitt Artillery to fire a salute from the battery on St.Cyre's Hill. He had had express notification of the battle, as Lieutenant-General in Command of the Forces along the South West Coast of England, but his neighbours had not and they were frightened by the gunfire, fearing the invasion had begun. More peacefully, Simcoe gave a great celebratory dinner at Wolford, with 500 lamps and a 61 foot table. The following year, he attended the State Funeral of Admiral Nelson, although it is recorded that he was late in arrival and there was no time to accord him his full military honours; that depressed the General considerably.

At the height of the scares, the government issued proposals "for rendering the Body of the People Instrumental to the General Defence in case of Invasion"; one idea was for a Corps of Guides on Horseback and another for "driving the Country within 15 miles of the coast", clearing out all people and cattle and naming rendezvous areas, all of which required good maps. The general and specific instructions for the clearing of Dunkeswell Parish make interesting reading. The Parish was to be split into two halves, with one half assembling at the Church and the other at Perry's Plot on the Bywood estate. There would have been many frightened people milling round the Church, clutching the recommended blankets and supplies of food for a few days but Constables and Churchwardens and the newly appointed Conductors and Overseers would have restored calm. The Sick and Infirm would have been directed to their appointed carts. One was to be provided by Robert Burrough, with Richard Burrough as Driver and Edward Salway as Conductor; the Conductor's passengers would have been notified already and they included two Simcoe children, Henry and Katherine, Mrs.Quin, Betty and Thomas Scadding, Rachel Burrough, Sarah and Betty and Samuel and Richard Salway and 10 other named persons. When all had been assembled, they were to set off on cross country journeys to Somerton,via Castle Neroche, Curry Mallet, Curry Rivel and Langport, or to Dartmoor, via Bradninch, Thorveton, Crediton,

Higher Wottem and Chagford or South Zeal. They were expressly ordered to leave the turnpike roads for the use of the military. Four men were ordered each to have a waggon and three or four horses ready for the public service; four others were to be Overseers of cattle and another four of sheep, with 12 to 15 year olds driving them. Edward Burrough and John Baker were deputed to "take Charge of the Dead Stock", being ordered to destroy "the Hay and Corn, and Cattle of all Descriptions, particularly the Horses not retained for public Service, and render useless all the unemployed Carts and Waggons, before you remove yourselves, but this step is not to be taken, unless in the last Extremity". It was comforting to know that such detailed orders had been given, although they were never tested in practice.

Such movements would, hopefully, have been defended by regular and militia forces and it is from this time that came the sword found in the thatch at Fishponds House. It was originally thought to be a weapon tucked away after the Monmouth Rebellion, when for a man to have a sword was a dangerous thing and an invitation to appear before The Bloody Assize. The sword proved to be a 1796 Pattern Cavalry Sword, one which was used in the British Army between 1796 and 1821 and issued to Yeomanry Cavalry units at the time of threatened invasion; actually made in Germany, it had Devon Light Dragoons stamped on the blade, a general term for the Devon Yeomanry, a unit of which would have been raised in the Dunkeswell area and exercised locally. The dented edge to the blade shows that it had been used for the prosaic work of hedging or cutting wood.

Military matters always figured high at Wolford at that time and justified the crest of the Simcoe coat of arms being "A dexter arm in armour embowed holding a sword or" - an armoured, bent right arm, in its natural colours, holding a golden sword. The General's father was Captain John Simcoe, R.N., who had been an active serving officer, with an interest in land and sea warfare. He had been taken prisoner by the French in N.America in the Seven Years' War, 1756-63, sent up to Canada and released after six months; having seen the St.Lawrence River, he charted it and was sent to escort General Wolfe to Quebec but he died on the way, in May, 1759. The General's wife was the daughter of Colonel Thomas Gwillim, 50th Regiment of Foot, who had been Wolfe's Brigade-Major at the battle on the Heights of Abraham. Wolfe had died there, at Quebec, but the Colonel returned, although he did not live to see the birth of his daughter, Elizabeth Posthuma. Her mother died days after the birth and the girl found a substitute family in that of her aunt, in Hembury Fort House, and her husband, Admiral Graves, who had seen action in the War of American Independence.

Elizabeth's future husband had been in the Army since 1770, when he became an Ensign in the 35th Regiment of Foot. He served in America, commanding a Company of the 40th Regiment of Foot, was severely wounded at the battle of Brandywine in 1777, commanded the Loyalist Queen's Rangers, was captured in an ambush in 1779 and held for six months, eventually being invalided home in 1781, due to "excessive fatigue and vexation", as The Gentleman's Magazine put it in an obituary notice in 1806. Marriage, the start of a family and his organisation of Wolford estate did not entirely satisfy him and he yearned for high command. This came shortly after the birth of Francis Gwillim Simcoe in 1791 and he and Elizabeth spent five years in the vigorous Lieutenant Governorship of Upper Canada, the province with which his name was always to be linked. An abortive Governorship of San Domingo and unsuccessful attempts to secure the Governorship of Canada and a peerage meant his public service career was virtually over by 1798. His command in the South West left him dissatisfied and at odds with Prime Minister William Pitt, although he was made a full General in the British Army in 1801. Despite brooding over his career prospects, the General tackled home defence with vigour. When he enclosed land in Dunkeswell, he agreed to make roads for military purposes. He had carpenters ready to cut down trees to block an enemy's progress, created a system of furze beacons, made a large camp for his forces at Woodbury Common and a strong battery on St.Cyre's Hill, with room enough for 200 guns. He organised sham battles for his regular forces, such as the 1804 one when an "English" army defeated the "French" encamped on Hembury Fort, and the Honiton Volunteers exercised on the Wolford Estate.. He co-ordinated the movements of his 50,000 volunteers in Devon and despatch riders regularly galloped to Wolford Lodge with the latest war news. He even made his estate workers march to and from work, behind a drummer, to inculcate fighting spirit into them. In 1806 came hope of more active work and he was made Commander-in-Chief in India; before taking up that position, he sailed with Earl St.Vincent to Portugal, to report on the need for aid there. It may have been the preparations made by the Navy to impress its passengers on HMS Illustrious that killed the General; the ship and her quarters had been newly painted and doctors ordered ship and General home when he was affected by the toxic smell of the new paint. From Torbay he went to Exeter and there died.

The funeral at Wolford in November, 1806, was a grand affair, with full military honours. From Exeter, three mourning coaches followed the hearse and its escort of the 3rd Dragoon Guards, the General's carriage and his horse with his boots reversed in the stirrups and his arms on the saddle, led by one of the Dragoon Guards. The Exeter Regiment of Volunteers assembled at 3 Mile Cross, outside Exeter, other Volunteer Regiments lined the road to Honiton, the General's own East Devon Yeomanry Cavalry were on the battery at St.Cyre's Hill and flaring torches lit the way at Wolford and at the funeral itself, lending a touch of high drama to the proceedings. Minute guns had been fired in Honiton and the Luppitt Company of Artillery fired a final salute, which shook Wolford Lodge.

The General's military prowess lived on in his son, Francis; an Ensign in the 27th (Inniskilling) Regiment of Foot in 1807, he was sent in the same year to Wellington's Peninsular campaign, to Corunna and then to the two sieges of Badajoz. The Parish registers record that "Francis Gwillim Simcoe, Esq., Lieutenant of Grenadiers 3 Battalion 27th Rgt of Foot, eldest son of John Graves Simcoe, Lieut General, late of Wolford Lodge, in the Parish, deceased, and Elizabeth Posthuma his wife, was killed bravely fighting in the breach at the storming of the City of Badajoz, in Spain, in the month of April, 1812, in the 21st year of his age 'Dulce et decorum est, pro Patria mori.'". The Latin tribute, that it had been sweet and graceful to die for one's country, was a sincere memorial to him in the days before the horrors of the First War trenches made such words a mockery.

Two years later came a cessation of fighting and Napoleon's first exile. Dunkeswell celebrated in style. Whereas the fiftieth anniversary of the accession to the throne of George III had been marked by a service, ringing of the bells and the distribution to the poor of roasted sheep, bread, potatoes and a hogshead of cider, the Peace was celebrated by rich and poor alike. There were floral arches, a band and singing, special items by the schoolchildren, a service of thanksgiving and a great dinner of beef and pudding, at which two hogsheads of cider were consumed; the Vicar wrote with relief that the whole had been "conducted with the utmost order and harmony", a Dunkeswell characteristic that has come through to the present day. Peace did not mean that England could entirely relax and the men of Dunkeswell were still required to register for the Militia and to serve, unless they were specially exempted. In 1817, Parish Constable Edward Salway listed 72 men between the ages of 18 and 45 in his return to the County, and his list was socially revealing. John Pyle was exempted from service because he was in the Army Reserve already; aged 39, the farmer had seven children under the age of 14. Another one also in the Reserve was William Burrough; aged 41 and a farmer, he also had seven children under 14. However, John Webber, thatcher, aged 40, with six children under 14, had to serve.

No.50 on the list was James Pike, Labourer, aged 32, who was exempted "as a Poor Man"; his six children under 14 were subsidised by the old Poor Law. An 18 year old bachelor cordwainer, John Wood, was exempt because he had become an "Apprenticed Licensed Teacher not carrying on a trade". Because the threat of rebellion by the dissatisfied never materialised in Devon, the Militia was not called into action and it was eventually replaced by the volunteers of the Territorial Army of the early twentieth century.

No record exists of Dunkeswell men who might have enlisted for the Boer War, 1899-1903, but the framed roll of honour in the church of those who went to war between 1914 and 1918 lists 42 men from the village who "served their King and Country". Family connections were strong between them; three Clays, Hansfords, Richards and Spillers are there, two Ashfords, Cannifords, Corricks, Dowells, Merchants and Wynnes. The First War was one of high casualties, particularly in the trench warfare of the Western Front, and three men did not return. Sergeant Robert George Hansford, born in Dulverton and enlisted in Exeter, was one of the 8th Battalion of the Devonshire Regiment which was committed to the battle of Loos on 15th September, 1915; he had fought in France and Flanders and was reported missing on 19th September, to become one of the 50,000 casualties which the British suffered in the month long fight. The horror of that battle meant many simply vanished, blown to pieces or buried in the mud, and their bodies were never recovered. The fates of the other two were more certain; Gunner Frank Tottle was killed at Arras, in April, 1917, while with his

Royal Field Artillery battery in support of the first co-ordinated attack by tanks, and Private Henry Irwin Merchant, of the 4th Wiltshires, died in Tidworth Hospital, in December, 1917, from wounds or illness. In all, Dunkeswell was fortunate that fatalities were not higher; as related elsewhere, the Second War claimed only one life from Dunkeswell.

The School Log Book of 11th November, 1918, recorded the emotions of the time; "It being reported that the Germans have signed the Armistice, the National Anthem was sung and cheers were given for the King and for our Army and Navy." The children contributed to a banner for Sir David Beatty, the dashing naval commander, and all signed a paper to go with it. The reality of Peace led to more singing of the National Anthem in 1919 and George V granted Dunkeswell and all other schools a whole week's holiday, to celebrate. Thereafter, the Dunkeswell School children regularly observed Armistice Day, with its two minute silence on 11th November.

One curious reference in the Parish Council minutes of September, 1918, stated that "It was proposed that the Clerk should write to the Superintendent of Police at Honiton, asking for increased Police supervision in the Parish, owing to the large number of Portugese (sic) labourers now residing in the Parish, especially as the licensee of the Royal Oak is a woman." Why Portuguese labourers were in the village is very unclear, although there are memories that they cleared woodland and stood in for men who had been called up for military service; that they were Portuguese is also disputed by claims that they were Ukrainians, perhaps refugees from the 1917 Russian Revolutions and the seizure of power by the Communists. The actual licensee of the Royal Oak had been called up and his wife had taken over the pub. There is no information about whether or not increased Police supervision occurred; there were no reports either of lawlessness or when the foreign labourers left the Parish.

In the recent Gulf War, it was the Airfield Industrial Estate which contributed to the success of the Allies; Supacats, originally from Hemyock, developed highly versatile vehicles which had important civilian uses but could also carry men and supplies across unfavourable country, such as the desert terrain of the conflict. The Ministry of Defence uses the high ground for communications purposes and military training still takes place in Dunkeswell, a reminder of the past.

Chapter 8

The Second War

There was little in the summer of 1939 to indicate that a great change would soon come to the village. True, the rumblings of war had been in evidence for the last two years and, in 1937, a Colonel Ramsden had come to explain the Air Raid Precautions system to a Parish Meeting and been thanked by the Council Chairman, Thomas H.Canniford. Parish Council meeting minutes, however, betray little anxiety and the outbreak of war in the September had occasioned no comments. Men and women had gone into the Services and it was with sorrow that Dunkeswell heard that 23 year old Arthur James Richards, a Private in the Devonshire Regiment, had been killed in an air raid on Plymouth, in July, 1940, the only fatal casualty from within the Parish; his body was brought back for burial by the Church gate. As in the First War, the village was most affected by the loss of farm labourers. They were gradually replaced by stalwart Land Army girls, many of whom found the reality of country life far removed from their own experience, and volunteers who had responded to Devon County War Executive Committee's appeal in May, 1940, to serve under a Parish Council appointed leader.

Evacuees came and swelled the numbers in school, so that the Parish Room again held pupils and the wooden hut by the Rectory was another overflow room for the London Evacuee Unit School, which was checked regularly by its own LCC Inspectors. When bad weather and lack of heating caused problems, then the two Schools merged, as in early 1942, when for three consecutive days the temperature in the Rectory Room never rose above 44 degrees Fahrenheit. The merger caused some equipment to be put into store in George Stevens's barn, including 19 shinty sticks and an abacus, while the woodworking tools went, appropriately enough, to Carpenter's Cottage, to be stored by Mr.F.H.Wells. Some evacuees, of course, soon returned to London, away from the strangeness of the countryside. In 1940, Jack Wakely left Rosemary Cottage and returned to Harrow; Henry and Ronald Planson went back from Knapp Cottage to Tooting; Arthur Daley from

Fishponds to Southwark; Doris Glasby from the Wolford Barn went home to Stepney and Rosemary Fifoot from Stentwood to central London. One girl evacuee was still at Hillside in 1942, when she wasted Police time by claiming she had been struck by a man on her way home; it turned out that she had fallen over and was worried about damage to her rationed clothes.

In June, 1940, Alfred Le Marchant organised a scrap metal collection and George Lane offered temporary storage for the bits and pieces, outside the Forge in the main street; later, there were many complaints about scrap piles being left uncollected and becoming nuisances. With Police co-operation, a Local Defence Committee was formed and headed by Mr.Paton in 1941; earlier appeals had elicited only two volunteers for Fire Watching and in 1942 there was a call for two Auxiliary Fire Servicemen in Dunkeswell. The Home Guard paraded and drilled and wanted the use of the Parish Room for training, later in 1942, but the lack of blackout in the room prevented its occupation, so the Guard turned to the Rectory. As part of Home Guard active service, members were sent to secure the railway tunnel by Honiton and keep an eye on bridges and any strangers. Those who were children at the time remember making camouflage nets and pullthroughs for rifles. Several of them acted as Home Guard messengers. The Parish Room had been used as a free canteen for members of the Forces but had had little use; when troops came to Dunkeswell, they were too busy with training. The School Headmistress, Phyllis Riddell, realised how attractive soldiers were to her pupils; on 10th February, 1941, she recorded that Leonard James Procter had cut his knee on a sharp stone in the playground, which required three stitches from Dr.Griffin that evening. The accident happened when the children were allowed outside in the afternoon so that they could watch "a sham fight by soldiers". A strict record of resident Aliens was kept by P.C.George Davis and he kept a careful eye on a Russian family which arrived in 1940; Isaac Obermeister, a watchmaker, his wife Mina and daughter Fanny lived at Hill View until they moved to Hemyock the following year.

P.C.Davis was also busy checking blackout regulations; one Honiton driver was cautioned and two local men fined 10/- each in 1940 for unscreened lights on their vehicles and a bonfire at Jenwood Farm in 1943 had to be doused lest it was visible to enemy aircraft. At a time when invasion was very much expected, in 1941 and 1942, five local men were cautioned or fined for failing to immobilise motor vehicles which might have aided an invader. At the same time, the authorities believed that any invader would be unable to read a map so all signposts were taken down and many milestones uprooted lest they send the German army on its line of advance. Perhaps the lack of signposting distracted the drivers of the defending forces even more. A close check was kept on the proper use of petrol and various cases came up in court where agricultural fuel had been misused. Yet another duty fell to PC Davis in 1940, when he had to arrest a deserter from the 37th Searchlight Unit at Tewkesbury; the man had been reported at a local farm and he was handed over to the military authorities. There was also the curious case, in 1949, when an escaped Czechoslovakian Prisoner of War was arrested in the Parish; that was some four years after the war in Europe had ended.

Then, at Christmas, 1941, the reality of total war came closer to Dunkeswell's 300 population ; Wimpey was given the task of constructing an RAF airfield on the plateau above the village on land requisitioned from local farmers, from the Burroughs at Southayes, the Sparkes at Hookedrise, the Lockes at Westhill, the Stevens at Slade and the Haymans at Hutshayes, with Percy, Cox's Hill and Jenwood Farms all surrendering land for the domestic quarters. To Dunkeswell came a coachload of Irish labourers, the advance party, to build hutted accommodation for the main body of some four hundred, again mainly Irishmen. They spent an unhappy festive season although villagers offered hospitality as best they could; the Smart family, only recently arrived as refugees from the bombing of Croydon and living in Bottom Cottage, went to the building site office with gifts, for example. The village pub was hard put to it to keep up with the demand for ale and stout; milk sales at Connetts Farm and local cider sales rose dramatically. So, too, did the crime rate. The Camp Commandant, the Welfare Manager, an Inspector, a clerk and a labourer all appeared before Honiton Magistrates in April, 1942, charged with being in illegal possession of clothing coupons and transferring them to unauthorised persons; fines were of £1 and £2, with 10/- costs. In the same year, an Irish worker stole food valued at £14.13.2 from the canteen, an electric drill found its way into the Mill stream, two sets of equipment vanished and a young worker received a three month Borstal term for another theft from the Wimpey site. A local man was fined £5, with 10/- costs,

Off-duty USN personnel meeting the people (USN Official Photo.)

and bound over for two years for taking two pairs of Wellington boots; unknown thieves made off with GPO material and, even, a wooden GPO telegraph pole.

However, the airfield emerged from the mud and rain and was allocated to RAF Bomber Command, only to be transferred to Coastal Command in April. There was one German air raid on the construction site, at 0955 hours on 26th October, 1942, when a solitary aircraft dropped four bombs, causing minor damage to a runway and the taxi track but no casualties; one of the bombs failed to explode and was dealt with by the Bomb Disposal Squad. There had been two earlier alarms; on 23rd April, one bomb at Abbey Mill Farm caused some damage to the farmhouse and Holy Trinity Church; three days after that, two bombs fell on the Turbury and Manor Farm; neither exploded and the Bomb Disposal Squad removed them. However, the possibility of heavy bombing of the aerodrome area encouraged the Parish Council, in April, 1943, to order a temporary mortuary to be created in the Chapel garage.

When German submarines moved out of the Channel, the advantages of Dunkeswell airfield were limited until, in August, 1943, it was made over to the United States. First to fly in were Liberators of the 479th U.S.Army Air Force Anti-Submarine Group, on 6th August, with four Squadrons in all by the 19th, under the operational control of 19th Group Coastal Command. Then, in September, 1943, the U.S.Navy took over, Fleet Air Wing 7, on the only USN base on British soil. Technically still an RAF station and guarded by the RAF Regiment until its full Commissioning as a U.S. Naval Facility on 23rd March, 1944, under Commander Thomas Durfee, USNR, it became home for never less than three and a half thousand American sailors, with their Liberator and Catalina aircraft. Lt.Commander Charles A.Hall said that "a man grows to love his ship, whether it's in mud or water", but that was when he was leaving "Mudville Heights" in April, 1944. Living, working and flying conditions must have been hard, especially when the accommodation on the Highfield area and the military end on the airfield were unfinished; even when finished, there must have been a sense of isolation and strangeness which, perhaps, occasioned one young Ensign from Ohio to commit suicide in January, 1944, a heavy blow for his wife at home in Berea. The USN authorities did their best to arrange entertainment for their men, to combat any homesickness;

one of the stars they flew in was the great Joe Louis, who gave a boxing exhibition.

Local people came to welcome the Americans, despite the strangeness of the Royal Oak accepting dollars and dimes from American personnel when the sailors eventually reached the head of the pub queue. One much remembered by the USN was "Granny" Rose Driver, who lived in Church Cottage; she and Reg entertained many Americans and enjoyed their company, even when the temptation of Reg's cider barrel was too much for them and they removed it by truck. Pigs were also a great delicacy for them, when they could round up one or two. There is a delightful photograph of the time, part of a set of USN propaganda photos for use at home, showing some Americans outside Connetts Farm, chatting to a young wife and her baby, and another of Navy personnel queueing to use the red telephone box by the thatched Post Office; the box is now a Listed building and a potent memory for returning Veterans. The Americans were a great success with the children, especially when they threw sweets over the school playground wall and made the teacher blush, to the delight of her charges. Children went up to parties at the airfield and to the cinema while girls from the area were brought in to attend the dances, with special passes to get them by the sentries who ringed the village. Some Americans married girls from the area, but there were only a few weddings in St.Nicholas's Church itself. In the early war years, as in the rest of Britain, there had been a rash of weddings, with five couples being wed in 1940 and four in 1941; then, in 1944, three out of four bridegrooms were from the base, a Lieutenant, a Sergeant and a Corporal, with a Flight Lieutenant of the Royal Canadian Air Force being the only bridegroom in 1945. The official paperwork to allow these weddings was considerable. Church and Chapel welcomed the Americans of all denominations and the Church was the recipient of post-war generosity, in the form of its organ and a later improvement of it.

The RAF/USN base was declared a Protected area and military and civilian police were active in guarding it. In particular, the local constable checked that all workers on the base, mainly from Eire, had residence permits, and he was busy turning away people who had no right to enter Dunkeswell. It was surprising how many young ladies claimed that they were coming to visit relatives, especially the licensee of the Royal Oak, who was everybody's "uncle". In 1944, the constable cautioned a domestic servant from Fancy Farm, when she tried to get on to the Base; he next arrested a sixteen year old girl from Middlesex and Honiton Magistrates bound her over in the sum for £50 until she reached eighteen. A man from Culmstock made two attempts to enter and was sent away with a caution; he was later arrested in Taunton, on a charge of larceny.

American driving and heavy trucks and jeeps combined ill with the Dunkeswell roads and the metal posts outside Corner Cottage, reduced in height in 1966 because they were so unsightly, testify to the need to protect vulnerable buildings. Mrs.Mary Middleton had twice to report vehicles crashing into Corner Cottage wall, once in 1943 (an RAF lorry) and again in 1944 (a USN truck). Amongst the fatalities from the airfield were three killed in a road accident outside Honiton, on 21st June, 1944, three more in a truck out of control in Exeter on the same day and one killed in a jeep on 9th May, 1944. In 1944, the School came in on a Monday to find the playground wall had been damaged by an American vehicle which had failed to take the sharp corner; perhaps it was the breach in the wall that led two boys to run away that lunchtime. In 1943/45, at least twelve other accidents were reported in which USN vehicles were concerned; they hit hedges and telegraph poles, other lorries, William Allen's 14 year old mare cob at Southayes and a bay horse at Jenwood Farm, Robert Stevens's car on the Abbey Road and Combe Cottage. The Devon Education Authority was so worried about the dangers to school children that it wrote to the Base Commander, deploring the speed with which vehicles went up and down Mill Hill and Fancy Hill. As late as 1949, the new owner of Percy Farm, W.G.Gollop, was claiming compensation for the damage USN vehicles had caused to his buildings. Vehicles attached to the RAF Regiment at the aerodrome and at the wireless station on Wolford Farm, near Limers Cross, were not much better. In 1943 a Chevrolet lorry met an RAF jeep on Chapel Cross, injuring one RAF man and three WAAFs. Early on the morning of 27th November, that year, a Squadron Leader, driving a lorry on the Turbury Road, killed an RAF cyclist. They continued after the end of the war, too; in 1946, two RAF lorries became jammed on a narrow part of Percy Hill and, in 1948, a troop carrier hit a car in the village street.

Other dangers might sooner have come from the ring of anti-aircraft guns round the base and falling shrapnel but the guns were never in serious action. They were, perhaps, more dangerous after the war when some of their buried ammunition was dug up, as by young Jonathan Froggat in the garden of Little Tencery in 1974. On the airfield itself, some workmen suffered leg injuries in 1950, when a steel purlin hit and exploded a buried bomb. In 1965, Bomb Disposal experts removed a suspected bomb from the airfield and blew it up.

The USN was also very active in scrutinising passes and challenging intruders. On 10th November, 1943, the proprietor of the Angel Hotel, Honiton, had the unpleasant experience of being fired on while driving along Southayes Lane at 2315 hours, with damage to his petrol tank; the USN admitted liability. In July the next year, civilian police had occasion to report "the unsatisfactory (but unspecified) behaviour of US Military Guards at their Piquet Posts".

The work of the Wing was valuable and greatly helped to reduce the threat of U-Boats in the Bay of Biscay and the approaches to the Channel. Constant low level patrolling, with aircraft often taking off at two hourly intervals, in all weathers, meant the enemy submarines could not easily rise to travel on the surface, hoping to conserve their fuel and make better time. Some aircraft never got very far. In one case, on 23rd October, 1943, a Liberator VPB105, took off from the airfield, in a westerly direction, loaded with depth charges; for some reason, the pilot, Lt.John C.Hillman, USNR, of New York, was unable to prevent sudden loss of power and the 'plane crashed half a mile from the airfield, just north of Turbury Cross, and all ten of the crew were killed in the huge explosion that followed.

Men who flew from Dunkeswell recall the many times when their aircraft had to be diverted, to Wales, St.Eval, St.Mawgan, Chivenor or Beaulieu for example, rather than face the hazards of returning to base in low cloud and fog, with darkness and icing of wings. There were directional indicators, such as the DW on field 275 at Bywood, sometimes illuminated at night, but they were easily obscured. Lt.William Wells Parish, from Lebanon, Tennessee, and his crew of nine all died when their Liberator crashed into high ground near Okehampton in bad weather. Don Dirst, an ex-Radioman, recalled that his crew often had to ask, "Where may I land ?", and that one hazard was the weakness of radio signal strength. Aircraft that had to ditch in the sea did not always receive help; Lt.George William Brown, of Iowa, and his crew of seven crashed into the sea on 10th September, 1943, and were lost. Others were listed as missing in action when aircraft failed to return from patrol; Lt.Thomas R.Evert, from Wisconsin, and his crew of nine on 22nd October, 1943: Lt.William Edward Grumbles, from East Greenwich, and his men on 8th November, and others in 1944 and 1945.

On St.Valentine's Day, 1944, a Liberator of VB103 took off at 0735 on a routine anti-submarine patrol over the Bay of Biscay, under Lt.K.L.Wright. All went well until 1634 hours when, with the aircraft at a height of 3000 feet, a radar contact showed two enemy aircraft three miles away. The aircraft were JU188s which came out of the clouds below the Liberator and their leader opened fire at a range of 1200 yards, registering many hits on the Liberator; the fire was returned from bow and top turrets and the starboard waist gun, recording hits on the German 'plane. Although the Liberator gained cloud cover almost immediately and the JU188s did not pursue the combat, enough damage had been done for No.4 engine to smoke and No.1 engine to be out of action. The bomb load was dropped and a course set for Dunkeswell; the aircraft was hard to fly and, when No.4 engine went out at 1800 hours, Lt.Wright had to ditch. Despite his skill, the aircraft broke into two and remained afloat for only five or six minutes. None of the crew had been injured by enemy action but the Radiomen, Thomas Edwin Ryan of Kentucky and Robert Charles Erdman of California, were trapped in the sinking 'plane. Binnie Faubion of Oklahoma was severely injured internally and, although he escaped through the port waist hatch, he died in the dinghy. The survivors were eventually spotted by other aircraft, which dropped a dinghy and emergency rations to them, and they were picked up at 1315 on 15th February by a British Air-Sea Rescue launch and returned to England. The report on the crash stated that the crew had conducted themselves "with courage and showed excellent discipline", noted that the firepower of the JU118s was superior and recommended some modifications to training and life saving equipment; the crew's chilled hands had made them lose the large raft because they could not grasp the handles. So were lost three out of 183 officers and men who died on active service, are commemorated on the plaque inside the Church and remembered with gratitude at the USN Memorial Service every summer in Dunkeswell.

Losses of men and aircraft were heavy; for example, two aircraft were lost on 22nd October, 1943, one on 26th February, 1944, and another on the 27th. Two more went down in March and two on 1st April, 1944. Another two followed in August and one in September, with the final loss on 14th January, 1945, of Lt.R.D.Spalding of New Hampshire and ten others. The aircraft lost on 27th February, 1944, had taken off after learning of the loss of the other Liberator on the 26th; it was to fly along the south coast of Ireland, to search for UBoats, but crashed into the tiny island of Skellig Michael, off the coast of County Kerry, with the loss of all eleven crew. That loss has recently been thoroughly examined by the Warplane Research Group of Ireland. Other 'planes and men were lost whilst being ferried to and from the States, as on 28th December, 1943, when a Liberator from Dunkeswell disappeared with twelve men on its way to America.

Casualties were not confined to the USN; on 19th October, 1943, Aircraftsman Cane, of 2854 Squadron, RAF Regiment, was accidentally shot dead while helping to guard the airfield; a .303 bullet from an Enfield rifle was accidentally discharged by a fellow Aircraftsman, Horace Harding. A few days earlier a Wellington bomber of 547 Squadron, RAF, had crashed at Dunkeswell while on a transit flight, when a wing fell off; the USAAF pilot, four RAF crew and one RAF passenger were all killed.

Losses but successes, too, mainly in disrupting German plans. Lt.Parish, later killed near Okehampton, attacked a submarine on the surface in November, 1943, and merchant ships and a destroyer in December; Lt.Rudd attacked merchant vessels on the same December day and a submarine in the following January. Activity lessened after D-Day in June, 1944, as Western France fell into Allied hands and U-Boat anchorages vanished; sightings and attacks did continue, however, and a U-Boat was hit by a homing torpedo on 25th April, 1945, and a Dunkeswell aircraft received the first surrender of a U-Boat after hostilities ended, off the Scilly Isles, on 9th May.

Things moved swiftly at the end of the War in Europe; FAW7 HQ moved from Plymouth to Dunkeswell to the USA by the end of July and Dunkeswell became the base for an RAF Ferry Unit in August until March, 1946. In that period, there were further losses. A British Anson aircraft, PH822, was bound for Dunkeswell but crashed at Higher Grange Farm on 19th October, 1945; the pilot, Sergeant Wood, received severe facial lacerations and Pilot Officer Hooper fractured a femur.

The RAF men guarding the crash site were reprimanded for doing damage to an unoccupied building. A Warwick aircraft on a test flight on 9th November, 1945, came down in the Bristol Channel; the Pilot's body was never found but the body of the other occupant, Warrant Officer P.Hutchinson, was washed ashore on a beach in County Cork. On 16th December, 1945, a glycol leak caused one of the port engines of a Lancaster bomber to smoke; the action of feathering that engine led to a failure of the other port engine and a drastic loss of height, so that the ferry flight ended on a hillside near Mortehoe GWR station, with the death of Flight Lt. C.R.Booth, the pilot. In bad weather, in 1948, the airfield had to admit an Auster civilian aircraft, which managed a safe landing. The RAF finally gave up the airfield in February, 1949, and it was available for civilian use by the Gliding Club and then the Dunkeswell Aero Club in 1967. RAF planes still used the airfield and, on 16th February, 1954, a Vampire of 208 Advanced Flying School hit the ground with its starboard wingtip and crashed, killing Pilot Officer R.W.Mall.

Some American equipment was left behind, much of it having been wrecked and buried and now being rediscovered by local enthusiasts, some went back to the States and some was given away; for several years after the War, when it rained, "you would see the raincoats coming out with US Navy on the back". The temptation of all that USN and RAF equipment proved too much for some; in 1944, information received led the police to a store of USN food in a Luppitt cottage. In 1946, an RAF man received a sentence of six months on three charges of stealing RAF clothing and a knife and a civilian was fined for removing nine chairs and four complete wheels from two Air Ministry fire engines. In 1948, there was another police sweep which netted several men who had stolen or received RAF property, landing them with heavy fines or gaol sentences. A steady drip of Air Ministry and Home Office material followed; eight doors and frames and 2 cwt of brass scrap vanished in 1948, three men were caught loading seventeen stirrup pumps on to their van, and four lorries were seen on the airfield, loading up stolen goods in 1949. There was, however, a lighter side to misdeeds. In May, 1946, Isaac Evans of Jenwood reported that one of his hay ricks had gone up in smoke; on investigation, Constable Denithorne recorded that "the outbreak apparently caused by RAF personnel using the rick for 'courting purposes' dropping lighted match or cigarette". There was the same type of suspicion aroused in 1949 when 60 or 70,000 "biscuits" (coir fibre and flock square mattresses so disliked by servicemen) in one of the hangers were destroyed by fire, although the official report was "Spontaneous Combustion".

The history of the USN in Dunkeswell would not, of course, be complete without the story of Lt.Joseph Kennedy, brother of President John F.Kennedy, and his co-pilot, Lt.Wilford T.Willy, of Fort Worth, Texas. The two men had served at Dunkeswell before volunteering for a special mission, the purpose of which was to destroy V1 and V2 and long range gun silos near Calais, which had been creating devastation in England. They had a new Liberator from the States converted into a huge bomb, to be escorted by two "mother ships", PV1 Venturas, and other aircraft, setting a course from Fersfield aerodrome in Norfolk at 1752 on 12th August, 1944. The aircraft flew over Framlingham, Suffolk, at 1815, then the Liberator was turned by one of the Venturas and headed towards Beccles. The two pilots were to have ejected from the Liberator over the coast; the 'plane would then have been taken on, to descend almost vertically into the German concrete emplacements. Unfortunately, the Liberator exploded over the Suffolk countryside, killing both men and showering wreckage over a large area, much of it in New Delights Wood at Blytheburgh. Perhaps the electrical circuitry of the aircraft was at fault, perhaps an unlucky radar signal from Dunwich or Darsham caused the detonation. In the 1980s, there were claims made by a Luftwaffe Officer that a Joseph Kenedy had been shot down in Normandy in the July and that he and a fellow officer had been shot while trying to escape, but that may have been an attempt by another American to secure better treatment by adopting the Kennedy name. There was no confirmation of the affair from any other source.

Two footnotes to the years when the Americans were in Dunkeswell. German paratroopers did manage to drop on the airfield, in considerable numbers, but that was for the 1976 production of the film, "The Eagle has landed". The only reference to the USN presence in the village in the Parish Council minutes was an indignant squawk in February, 1945, that "the Drome people are emptying their sanitary buckets close to the road towards Dunkeswell Abbey"; they may have been the squatters who were troublesome later but the presence of squatters on a USN base seems unlikely. The villagers, however, remembered their allies with affection and some considerable pride and overlooked some of their wilder moments, though Rhoda Blackmore and Lily Richards would recall the time when US personnel fired bullets through their windows. Every year, there is a memorial service to honour the Officers and Men of FAW7, those who served and those who died. To begin with, detachments of American and British Naval units attended each year, flying in to the airfield; now a representative of the USN comes down from the Embassy in London and he and the Chairman of the Parish Council together lay wreaths in front of the memorial plaque in the Church, in the presence of a large and mindful congregation. The Church Visitors' Book, under the American Flag presented by Douglas Luther, also contains the names of many USN Veterans who have returned over the years and who have always been sure of a great welcome from the village; they find great changes on the ground but clearly recognise the area from the air. Rosie Driver's words of what she felt in 1943 remain true to this day; "I saw some walking up the street and I just had to go out and speak to them." In the 50th Anniversary Service in 1993, the Rector asked the congregation to "remember that the wreaths are symbols of sacrifice made, thanksgiving for duty done and the alliance of two great nations, under God, and that this village was able to offer friendship and comfort to so many strangers". That friendship was reciprocated; in 1944, Norman L.Miller produced a little volume of poems and photographs of Dunkeswell and the Abbey, dedicated to Hedy and entitled "Somewhere in England"; the last poem ended ...

'Somewhere in England' will have an effect
When buddies meet up and help recollect
They'll all feel, I'm sure, as this land they depart,
There'll always be England locked up in each heart

Chapter 9

Agriculture

The main occupation of the people of Dunkeswell had always been on the land; the record of Domesday Book and later surveys of the Parish showed that agriculture provided a living although, for many, it may not have been a living much above subsistence level. The 6" to 1 mile map of 1887 marked a "Starve Acre Copse", near Gypsy Cross, and that must have been based on experience. In East Devon, it was the lusher valleys which yielded the good crops and were worked more thoroughly; the hill top culture or wood pasture of the Blackdowns had to contend with flinty, moory land, much covered with gorse and heather and a poor, slightly acidic soil. It led to an individual type of farming settlement, based around the old village but more widely dispersed as groups of settlers or squatters carved out for themselves areas on which to farm and, because they did that, they produced a society less cohesive than that of the valleys and lowlands.

The famous three field system could not have been fully implemented in the Parish and it was an area of early enclosure of fields into self-contained units, much by purchase or mutual agreement, so that the main period of Tudor enclosure hardly affected Dunkeswell. Of course, much enclosure had been done by the Abbey, from the thirteenth century onwards, either in the form of pastureland which would earn a steady income, or in the Granges. A Grange was an area of some two or three hundred acres centred on essential buildings and fenced, hedged or ditched to separate it from surrounding land; the great benefit of such enclosed land was that experiments could be tried by the Abbey and its servants and farming could be on a larger scale, especially with plough teams of eight oxen. Granges were established in Dunkeswell and neighbouring Parishes and may have occasioned the dispossession of some already on the land. The 1539 grant of Abbey lands to John Lord Russell included the Granges of Sheldon, Bowerhayes and Bywood; there was also Dunkeswell Grange. The Granges were managed by lay bailiffs but the essential policy was formed in the Abbey Chapter House which, in its turn, was influenced by the work of other Cistercian Abbeys, such as Waverley and Forde.

The Abbey also set up tenant farmers in messuages, or large farms, and tenements, the smaller holdings. The tenants either worked full time on their land and paid rent or worked for some time on the Abbey land in place of rent. Records from Powderham Castle, Exeter, probably from the Exchequer Augmentation Office dealing with Abbey lands in 1539, list some of the tenants and their tenancies. Several come under Olde Dunkeswell; John Onanleigh and two others held "a tenement called Sendcomer and some land called Le Strete on the north side of the tenement and land called Jameswood on the West side, Rent 67p."(1532); Agnes Serle and three others held a tenement and a field called Foteland (1532), while Jane Smythe and three others held the lease of Tencery and some other lands in the parish (1533). Others are under Bowerhayes Manor; John Junior Phillips held Pitplace (now Fancy Farm) and Rufgreylonde with right of pasture for 70 years and Stonifyledmede (1537), John Pococke had two tenements and one cottage at Huntshayes (1508) and William Serle and two others held an estate at Southayes (1537). Under Wolferchurche Manor, Jane Serle and two others held a close at Wolferchurche and the "More" there (1536) and, under The Grange, John, Thomas and Jane Serle held Wolferchurche Grange (1535). At the Dissolution of the Abbey in 1536, the Royal Commissioners assessed the rental value of lands at Dunkeswell to be £5, Bywood Grange, £3.6.7, Bowerhayes Grange £7.10.0 and Sheldon Grange £4.0.0, out of a total land value of £34.13.6. The Crown's Steward of the Manor of Dunkeswell had to make regular reports on the enclosed areas of land as well as the tenantry and his own stewardship. In 1622, William Palfrey, Steward of the Manor of Bowerhayes, made his report to the "Prince's Council" and asked that he be allowed fuel and wood in lieu of 36/8 arrears of salary due to him from the Crown.

The real period of Parliamentary Enclosure was in the late eighteenth century and early nineteenth, when Private Acts of Parliament enabled landowners to take over some of the unused and Common land. Commons were an essential part of the agrarian economy of the Middle Ages and later and they consisted of meadows, waste land and roadside verges on which Parishioners could graze their cattle, although any meadow was forbidden for grazing between Candlemas (2nd February) and Lammas Day (1st August), when it was cropped. Landowners often had rights over the Commons and the right to check that all cattle grazing on them belonged to those with Common Rights. In 1801, there was a General Enclosure Act (41 George III), to streamline the procedure, and many took advantage of the speedier processes of law. General Simcoe, being the chief landowner of the Parish, enclosed large areas, in stages. In 1801, a special Act for Dunkeswell stated that 1,500 acres of Commons and Waste Land "are of very little value" and "it would be of great Benefit to all Persons interested therein if the same were divided and inclosed". That enclosure appears in various Indentures, as for Mansell's; referring to land round the dwelling, it is described in 1817 as "lately inclosed from the Commons and Waste Lands in Dunkeswell" and in 1820 and 1835 there is confirmation that it was enclosed under the 1801 Act.

A Dunkeswell Inclosure Release of 26th March, 1803, between Enclosure Commissioners (two local gentlemen, Richard John Marker and Thomas Garnsey of Uffculme and a County Land Surveyor, William Bond of Axminster), John Scadding (Yeoman of Dunkeswell and the General's Agent) and John Graves Simcoe, Esquire, clearly defines land that was to be taken over by the General at that time. There were two parcels of land bounded by the road to Ewins Ash and the turnpike road from Honiton to Taunton, 21 acres and 25 acres, and another parcel of 25 acres on the eastern side of the others, "All which said several parts or parcels of land are parts and parcels of the Commons and Wastelands within the Manor and Parish of Dunkeswell aforesaid". The Act "for dividing allotting and inclosing all the Commons and - Wastelands within the Manor and Parish of Dunkeswell in the County of Devon" also gave all rights to the General, detailed as all ways paths passages waters watercourses easements profits commodities advantages and appurtenances whatsoever", for £770.

The land was used in three ways. Some was split up into 300 acre portions, reminiscent of the Abbey Granges, and made tenant farms, such as Wolford Farm; when Elizabeth Posthuma Simcoe, in 1845, leased the farm to "Henry White of Farway in the said County Yeoman .... and Thomas White of Colyton in the said County Carrier Brother of the said Henry White and John Madge of Gittisham in the said County Yeoman Brother in Law of the said Henry White", the farm was clearly described as "that Messuage Barton and Farm .... containing by

The Connetts Farm complex

Tencery Farmhouse

estimation three hundred and ten acres (more or less) now in the occupation of John Bishop as tenant", although it was down to 243 acres in the 1923 Wolford Estate sale. Manor Farm had also been reduced in 1923, down to 159 acres.

Other land was added to the Wolford Lodge Estate itself and the rest was given over to Plantations, in which the General indulged his love of arboriculture; some Plantations he created were Coronation, Turbury, Oak, Douglas, Blackdown, Roughborough, Roughgrey, Cleeve and Rowbarrow, which helped give work to any who may have suffered from the removal of the Commons, as well as providing timber and aesthetic improvement of the Estate. There were impressive amounts and varieties of timber sold in 1923. The Chase had 23 acres of Oak, Ash, Beech, Sycamore, Sweet Chestnut, Spruce, Birch, Elm, Cherry and Horse Chestnut, while Pen Point Wood was able to add Larch, Scotch Fir and Cedar. The Tithe Commutation Map of 1841 showed much land that was marked, ominously for the poor, "Land of Mrs.E.P.Simcoe, formerly Common". With the Enclosures went the creation of hedges and ditches round the fields and the straight roads, such as Long Lane, which acted as boundaries and also facilitated the movement of troops and artillery in event of a French invasion.

The strength of farming is shown by there being still a working farm, Connetts, in the middle of the village; the farmhouse was built in the sixteenth century, with additions in the seventeenth century, including the fireplaces, and the nineteenth. It stands within its own farmyard, split as it is by the road to the Post Office, and it and its outbuildings and its nineteenth century stone rubble wall are Grade II Listed Buildings. The farmhouse, of local stone rubble and cob (a mixture of clay and straw), may have started as an open hall house, especially as there are two full height stone rubble walls at each end of the centre two rooms, being heated by an open hearth fire. Adjoining rooms were added later and all the farmhouse windows are at the front; the main roof was thatched and the outbuildings had a later corrugated iron roofing. It was a compact, functional and aesthetically pleasing working unit and able to accommodate farm and house servants.

The other farmhouse in the centre of the village, just by the Church, has been converted into two dwellings, Bramble Cottage and Middle Tencery. Tencery Farm was in the possession of the Abbey from its inception and Jane Smythe was the last Abbey tenant, with her lease for life from 1533, since which time it was a working farm until its sale and conversion in the 1970s. In 1923, the Simcoe sale listed it as having a dairy, granary, workshop, 4 pigsties, calves' house, hackney stable, cow house, another stable, Dutch barn, waggon house, trap house and cider house, quite a comprehensive range of buildings grouped round its farmyard. The farmhouse was built at the end of the sixteenth century or in the early seventeenth, of stone rubble, and partly renovated in the nineteenth, with some brick dressings, stone rubble chimney stacks and brick chimney shafts, with a thatched roof. The hall and an unheated room were in Middle Tencery, the through passage, service area and kitchen being in Bramble Cottage. When the final conversion took place, the outbuilding attached to Middle Tencery was also converted into a dwelling and the cross passage threshing Barn was pulled down to ground level and three dwellings constructed on the foundations, in the form of the original barn but with the addition of a gantry well that was not on any of the early photographs. Maps show that here was another farm which had developed as a self contained unit although now its orchard bears the houses of Tencery Orchard and its garden Tencery Cottage. Both Tencery and Connetts display the strong qualities of the old farming and social systems.

Other farmhouses were situated near the village, such as Percy Farm, of the nineteenth century, Highwood and the late sixteenth century Fancy Farm. A Grade II Listed Building, Fancy Farm, or Pit Place, stood within its own farmyard, although the oubuildings in front of it have now gone; it was enlarged in the late nineteenth century and modernised in this century. Just beyond it are Coxes Hill Farm, of the late eighteenth century, and Southlands, a sixteenth/seventeenth century farmhouse, again with later alterations and Grade II Listed. Other nearby farms are Hutshayes, Slade, Knapp, Hookedrise, Southayes and the once imposing Bowerhayes, most important of the Abbey Granges but doomed to be burnt down early in this century. Others are those already mentioned near Wolford House, with a third group in the vicinity of the Abbey, such as Abbey Wood Farm, the late sixteenth century Abbey Meadow with later extensions and modifications (Grade II), Musgrove Farm from the late seventeenth century with alterations and additions through to the present day (Grade II), and Park Farm. Then, there is the ring of outlying farms, one of which earned mention in the Quarter Sessions of 1690. Bywood Farm had been taken over from the dissolved Abbey and formed part of the Manor of Dunkeswell; the trustees of the Manor had to go to court to gain the sum of "two and twenty pounds for 2 years of Rent owed at Michaelmas last past". The Court ordered that two men, Richard Searles and James Reeby, with other persons, should go to Bywood and take goods to the value of the missing rent; it allowed that the "said persons shall be saved blameless for what they shall lawfully do in the process".

The list of sixteenth and seventeenth century Devon Inventories contains only one for Dunkeswell, made on 8th February, 1554, by John Phylyppis and Peter Mychell of the goods of Margery Butte, "widow woman". Her possessions were agricultural and domestic and give some impression of that period. For livestock, she had 3 Kye (Kyne/cows), 4 boolockes, 2 yearlings, a horse and colt, 40 shepe and 2 peggis. Produce included 24/- worth of rye and otes, 3 bushelles of malte, 16/- of hay, 2 gallense of butter, 10 cheses, 10/- worth of byffe and bacon and 10 pounds of wolle. On the farm she had a payre harrasse to wagges (weights) of iron, a mattock, a pack saddell, 10 plankes of tymber and a delightfully named doungepecke. With domestic items such as vates and toubbys and 4 pannes of brasse, she was worth £16.18.6. She did, however, have some "detts that she dyd owe", to William Butte, Jone her daughter, Thomes Mathwe, Thomas Ley and Sir John Genynges, 33/8 in all.

Those farm labourers who did not live in separate cottages in the village or near the farms were accommodated in the farmhouses and treated much as family. In the 1851 Census, for example, the waggoner lived in at Dunkeswell Grange, three farm servants lived with the farmer's family at Southlands, two servants and two farm servants at Connetts and five servants (unspecified) at Fancy Farm. In 1861, Musgrove Farm accommodated a carter, dairymaid and ploughboy, Bowerhayes had two dairymaids and two farm labourers, Connetts had one dairymaid, a nursemaid and a ploughboy, Fancy Farm (named as Pit Place) was full again, Wolford Farm housed three farm labourers, a carter and a dairymaid and Persey (Percy) Farm held three farm labourers, a carter and a dairymaid. In the later Census reports, there are obviously fewer resident farm staff; Musgrove Farm was down to one agricultural labourer and one domestic servant in 1871, Southlands to one farm servant in 1881 and Wolford Farm only one domestic servant, although Abbey Wood Farm had a dairyman, dairymaid and agricultural labourer in residence. Generally, the slump in farming meant fewer workers were needed and they lived out when they could, especially in a period of earlier marriages.

The Census records of 1841 to 1891 inclusive show that agricultural labourers far outstripped any other class of occupation; the leaders were:

Agricultural labourers	275 recorded
Scholars	154
Farmers/landowners	146
Domestic servants	134

Agricultural labourers reached a peak in 1861, when 95 were recorded in the Parish, that being a considerable leap from the 34 of ten years earlier; numbers dropped away in the following decades, through 69 and 62 to only 40 in 1891. Perhaps they simply changed their job descriptions as numbers of farmers/landowners rose from 1841, when there were only 5, to a peak of 36 in 1881, dropping to 20 in 1891. 36 dairymaids/dairymen were listed but very irregularly, the ten yearly numbers from 1841 being 0, 0, 25, 4, 2, 5.

The full extent of agricultural occupation was displayed in the Tithe Commutation Map and Schedule of Titheable Land in Dunkeswell of 1841. The Tithe Commutation Act of 1836 (Commutation = exchange or substitution) had been necessary because of growing hostility to the payment of tithes to the Church of England; the farmers resented having to pay what they regarded as an extra rent, poor labourers felt they could spare nothing and hid some of what they had, the parishioners suspected that an Impropriator was making a profit and not paying the full amount to the incumbent, the incumbent himself found some of the tithes paid in kind were of poor quality or the runt of a litter and, of course, those who were outside the Church of England because they had no religion or were Nonconformists saw little reason to support the Established Church. To try to ameliorate the discontent, the Act converted Tithes into a Tithe Rent charge linked to the price of bread. It meant that, for the first time, a complete written and cartographic record of a Parish had to be made by Commissioners.

Late in 1841, William Blamire and Robert Jones, Commissioners, and Messrs Blackmore of Clayhidon, Solicitors, met the Impropriator of

Tithes in the Parish, Mary Graves, and the various Dunkeswell landowners. With them was William Summers of Ilminster, the Apportioner, who helped to decide how payments should be divided between various landowners. In all, 1158 acres 3 rods and 31 poles were divided; other land was declared exempt from Tithes as it had formerly been Abbey land, including Sheldon Grange and Inwood. The Commissioners eventually apportioned out a gross rent charge of £130, to go to Mary Graves. The surveying was accurately done and the final map, on a scale of 1" to 3 chains or 26.7" to 1 mile, was checked by a Royal Engineer officer, Lt.Dawson, at the Tower of London. The Dunkeswell Tithe map is not in a good state but can be viewed in microfiche form in the Record Office in Exeter. On the map, all the fields are numbered and the names are on the schedule.

Mrs.Elizabeth Simcoe was far and away the greatest landowner in the Parish, with, for example, 87 acres at Tentsery, 153 at Dunkeswell Grange, 147 at Southey and 376 at Byewood - the spelling is as on the schedule; with land at Wolford Church, Little Wolford, Manleys and Peckhays Hole, her holding was nearly 900 acres on which tithes had to be paid, and that was only part of the Wolford Estate. The other important owner of titheable land was the Revd.William Palmer, who had 109 acres at Hookedrise; smaller owners were John Rowe (79 acres at Hutshayes), Robert Burrough (41 at Southwell and Mansels), Mary Burrough (40 at Connotts) and John Melhuish (26 at Whitehorn or Coxhill), down to Sarah Dommett, with 12 poles at Rubens Castle. The schedule gives the names of the tenants of the properties; John Willey at Coxes Hill, Samuel Farrant at Connotts (he is also listed as owner), William Marks at Dunkeswell Grange, Robert Smith and Susannah Webber at Tentsery, Henry White at Byewood, Elizabeth Gossling at Manleys, etc.

The 257 listed fields are all marked as arable, pasture, meadow or orchard, with a collection of odds and ends, such as bog, garden or coppice. 120 fields are marked as arable, 37 as pasture and 22 as meadow. The field names range from the obvious to the obscure. Looking at John Rowe's land at Hutshayes, the names make sense; 5 Acres, Brooms Close, 3 Corners, 6 Acres, 5 Acres, Green Close, Home Orchard, Mow Barton, Buildings and Garden, Hill Croft Orchard and Rough Lands appear at the head of his field list. On the other hand, Robert Burrough Junior had a Dumkins Plot at Southlands, Elizabeth

Simcoe a Turnip Eddish (enclosure) at Wolford, William Marks a Tippity Close at Dunkeswell Grange, David Barton a Tipentale Orchard and a Rabbit Clapper 5 Acres at Southey and James Rosier a Buffy Close at Hookedrise. Interestingly, Field 108, farmed by Robert Smith of Tencery Farm, was called Football Field.

Many of the field names still survive, despite amalgamations of some of the smaller fields, but local agriculture in the twentieth century has mainly shifted from arable and mixed to low intensity livestock farming. Field amalgamation led to loss of hedgerows and that loss continues; the latest available figures are for 1972/3, when 1.75 kms or 5.4% loss occurred in the twelve months. However, the Parish is well hedged and the hedges well maintained, although the old but time-consuming skills of hand cutting and laying have often been replaced by machine cutting, which may lead to the creation of wide hedges, especially where they are part of old hedgebanks. In his book, "The Old Farm", Robin Stanes calculates that hedges take up one seventh of a hundred acre farm of four acre fields, that is some fourteen acres. The Devon hedgebanks provide shelter and impenetrable containment for animals, they are made up regularly and they enhance the landscape.

In 1911, F.J.Snell wrote about the Blackdowns and the "charming little villages, like Hemyock or Dunkeswell or Broadhembury, with their orchards fair and hollyhocks"; today, some hollyhocks but few "orchards fair". In 1841, the Tithe Map showed 21 orchards; for example, Dunkeswell Grange had Tippity Close, Great, Shut, Little, Young, Little Wood and Great High Pit Orchards and every farmer made his own cider, especially for his labourers' consumption. Most farms had a cider house, as Tencery did, and a cider press, as Bywood still has. In the 1871 Mortgage Indenture on four Wolford Estate farms, there were 4 orchards at Wolford Farm, 6 at Dunkeswell Grange and 1 at Manor Farm. Cider was a comparatively easy drink to make and, in the days when water was often impure, a safe drink; no water was used in its making and the acidity of apple juice and the effects of fermentation combined to kill impurities. The prevalence of cider making and drinking in Dunkeswell accounts for the lack of the alehouses which were so common in non-cider drinking villages. The "Royal Oak" has been the only public house in the main village, although there was one at Knapp, and the licensee of the "Royal Oak" in 1933, Charles King, made a complaint to the Police that cider was being sold at Knapp and undercutting his own trade. Cider may have been a strong seller to the USN personnel in the 1940s and often a snare to them but both production and demand had fallen since early this century. In the 1923 Wolford Estate sale, only eight orchards were included, three at Dunkeswell Grange and single ones at Tencery Farm, Garden Cottage (that now is), Lower Southayes and Wolford Farm. More tea, coffee and beer were being drunk, the water for their production had been boiled and there was more care taken with the monitoring of the local water supplies. Outside influences militated against cider making; the late nineteenth century Temperance Movement, the fact that farmers could not pay any of their labourers in alcoholic drink after an 1878 Act and the rise of cider making outside the West Country. Post-War Government grants to replace orchards with more profitable crops caused the final decay.

Dunkeswell had been very strict in looking after its orchards; the 1845 lease of Wolford Farm clearly stated what Elizabeth Simcoe expected from Henry White, that "he shall properly manure the orchards in each three years .... and shall plant with proper compost a good thriving young apple tree in the place of every apple tree which shall be decayed or blown down and shall preserve the same when planted from all injury and shall not stock the orchard with any cattle to injure the same and shall deliver up the orchard full planted and in good condition at the end of the said term ....". It also looked back to pagan times with its Wassailing ("Waes hal", Old English for "be of good cheer"), so that industry should be supported by superstition, a custom which has been revived in recent years. On "Old Twelfie", wassailers go round the village, not as "daily beggars that beg from door to door" but as "friendly neighbours whom you have seen before", bringing cheer, helping a good cause and receiving "warming from your excellent old ale". A supper of Witches' Soup and Witches' Pie at the Village Hall, an entertainment and a rehearsal of the ancient, midnight chant; then, to the "Old Apple Tree". In the glare of lights and to the ringing of the Church bells, sturdy witches are hooted and shot from the apple trees and a good crop ensured for the year, "whence thou mayest bear apples enow". In 1957, it was noted that 18 gallons of hot, spiced cider had been drunk; the Witches' Brew of country wines and secret ingredients is more popular today! The irony in 1994 was, of course, that such was the shortage of apple trees in the old village that the

Village Hall Committee actually had to buy a Bramley apple tree and plant it in the Playground so that the Wassailing ceremony could go ahead. What a decline indeed!

Not only was orchard culture regulated by Mrs.Simcoe but there were also clauses in the Wolford Farm lease about general agriculture. To fertilise the land, the tenant "shall bring upon every acre .... which he shall till 21 hogsheads of well burnt stone lime of the Blagdon Measure or 120 seams of well rotted dung or 1,000 seams of marl or such quantity of good manure as shall in the judgement of the said Elizabeth Posthuma Simcoe .... be equally beneficial". The number of crops taken each year should be regulated, with one "breaking crop before and two crops after such dressing". Land should be guttered and watered regularly, trees and hedges maintained properly and drainage works carried out. The Simcoes were enlightened landowners and Colonel Simcoe, as he then was, had attacked the 5,000 acres he bought in 1782 with vigour, especially after his choice of John Scadding as Farm Manager in 1784. In 1794 he wrote from Canada to ask Scadding to "cut down trees without mercy" where they interfered with the view from Wolford Lodge or blocked his farming plans. Scadding stayed at Wolford until 1817, when he left for a farm in Canada.

John Bailey, Wolford Lodge coachman, wrote about the Simcoes, in glowing terms; ".... to speak of the greatness and usefulness of General Simcoe is far beyond my power." He praised the Simcoes for their plantations and the amount of timber for sale; the construction of farm buildings through the Parish, such as barns and outbuildings at West Hill Farm and Southay; the erection of new cottages, such as Ball Nap Cottage and the cottages for John Tuck and William Dimond, and the conversion of Church Terrace from farmhouse to three dwellings; he urged his readers "to think of the new roads and hedges". He asked, "Was it by chance that General and Mrs.Simcoe came into the Parish of Dunkeswell ? No, the Lord ordained it to be so." John Bailey felt Isaiah's prophecies had been fulfilled, that "the mountains and hills shall break forth before you into singing and all the trees of the fields shall clap their hands". He had little reason to change his mind in his retirement in Percy Cottages (Autumn Cottage, now), before his death in 1855.

Today, much has changed and John Bailey would scarcely have understood present farming methods and organisation, the use of much sophisticated machinery and little hired manpower and the solitary life of the ear-protected man on the tractor in a distant corner of the farm. As late as 1935, Kelly's Directory picked out John D.Trenchard as a man of some importance, as he was a threshing machine owner. John Bailey would, however, feel that country life in Dunkeswell was well worth while.

Chapter 10

Trades and Occupations

The bodies of the murdered men lay in the Parish of Hemyock but the significance of their deaths lay in Dunkeswell. Walter and Adam had been killed by two strangers, Lawrence the Welshman and William the Welshman, who had then fled and escaped the King's justice. The year was 1239. The Abbot, the custodian of law and order on Abbey lands, had failed to report the crime and may have facilitated the escape of the murderers but it was a deed that could not be hidden and he was later in serious trouble, "in mercy" to the King's Justices, as was the Tything of Hemyock, "for not presenting the case as it should have done". How the Abbot extricated himself from that situation is not known but the power of the State over the Church may have been insufficient to reach a definite conclusion to the case.

The Welshmen were miners (the "fundatores" of the report to the Coroner) who had been brought to the Abbey to mine and smelt iron and it was the first reference to the iron industry in the Parish. It would not have been a large industry but a widespread and, perhaps, haphazard digging of iron ore from the sandstone and then smelting it in small, charcoal heated furnaces until enough pure iron was created for some of the needs of the Abbey. Today, the visible signs of iron are the brownish stainings of the water courses, as in the Dunkeswell Mill leat, from the iron oxide, and the lumps of slag that are dug up over a wide area, the fused impure iron and cinders from small furnaces; they are tangible and satisfying reminders of an age old industry.

The only other local mining about which anything is known was, also, over the Parish boundary, in Blackborough and Hembury; that was the whetstone mining in the "sandbeds" of the Blackdowns. The whetstones were the much valued sharpening stones needed by every agricultural labourer and others for sickles and scythes until they were replaced by the longer lasting carborundum stones, early in this century. The new stone put an end to the mining of whetstones, a process which had originated

Dunkeswell Mill

Carpenter's Cottage

in the seventeenth century or earlier. It is unlikely that Dunkeswell men were actively engaged in the actual mining, which was very much a closed shop, but they were purchasers of the whetstones which enabled them to hone the tools of their trade. Men were used to working in large groups, especially at hay and harvest times, and they were keenly critical of the skills of their fellows, whether cutting or hedging or ploughing, and their tools had to have both a competitive and actual edge to them.

The water power of the Madford Brook and River was utilised in Dunkeswell and at the Abbey. The earliest reference to a tucking or fulling Mill in Devon was to one at Dunkeswell, in a 1238 Assize Roll, while a similar mill was noted at Honiton six years later. The mill would have been by the Abbey as it was an integral process of the important woollen industry but needed sufficient capital to instal it, which only the Abbey would have had. When cloth was fulled or "tucked", as was the more usual term used in Devon, it was thickened, felted and smoothed by water and the rather smelly Fuller's Earth, a highly absorbent clay which would remove grease from the cloth. The process had been one of workers, the Fullers and Tuckers, actually "walking" the cloth but it was then revolutionised by the use of hammers tripped by water power. The Tucking Mill which appeared in the Census records of the nineteenth century was a reminder of the past, being occupied by a thatcher and a pauper and their families. It was here that "a monk of Dunkeswell, the keeper of the fulling mill at Dunkeswell, was crushed to death by the mill wheel". The report to the Justices in Eyre stated, "Misadventure. Value of the wheel 2/-." In an Indenture of 5th May, 1690, William Rawe of Dunkshill, Miller, and Mary Rawe, widow, his mother, granted to Richard Minifie, of Sarum, Wiltshire, "the Water Grist Mill commonly called the Abbey Mill", together with meadows called Mill Land, Little Mill Park and the Rodeing. Presumably, the Grist Mill was in addition to the Tucking Mill, as both Grist and Tucking names lingered on.

Old Dunkeswell, as the monks called it, had its own mill below Castle Field; it was not mentioned in the Domesday survey of the manor but must have come soon afterwards. The Devonshire Lay Subsidy of 1332, in which 11 men paid towards "great and arduous affairs in Ireland and elsewhere", was collected by James de Cokyngton and Matthew de Crouthorn. One payer was Richard the Miller (molendinarius) so he was a man of some substance. Other millers and owners can be traced back to Robert Phillips and two of his family, who had a lifelong lease of it from the Abbey at an annual rent of 27 pence in 1538. Later, it was owned by Alexander Marshall who died in 1692 and left the mill to his son, Thomas, and his daughter-in-law, Mary; they were aided by James Sheppard, recorded as a Gentleman, and Patience Humphrey, a widow. The mill passed through many hands, often being run by a consortium, with its members having other occupations as well as that of milling; in 1762, for example, there were Robert Arbury (yeoman or small farmer), his son-in-law, Samuel Salway (tailor) and James Bailey (miller); in 1797, three Somerset men ran it, Michael Bale (miller), Charles Core (Gentleman) and William Cowland who was, surprisingly, an Officer of Excise. The last miller was William Fricker, who kept the mill working until 1937. He gave great entertainment to village children by letting them walk on the stilts he had for walking in the flooded millfield. By then, though, it was a rebuilt mill for the old, thatched mill had been burnt down in the 1880s; the new mill used part of the old walls and was enlarged. It had two pairs of millstones and they were operated by the overshot waterwheel which took its water from the leat. The leat, or mill pond, was fed by the springs which come through where the sandstone hits the clay at the appropriately named Springfields and the water was contained in a long, narrow pond by a stone and earth wall on the south side. From there, it was taken under the road to a smaller pond, close to the mill, and fed onto the wheel through a wooden launder or funnel; there was also provision for an overflow channel. The watercourse can be clearly seen now, although the leat is smaller than it used to be and there is no mill machinery for the water to turn. From 1889, when John Hayward was both miller and baker, the miller often doubled up as baker, Edward Marshall in 1897, Gilbert Dave in 1900 and 1906 and the King Bros. in 1910.

The woollen industry was on a large scale in Devon and it was, for Dunkeswell, based round Honiton and the Culm Valley. As it was worked by cottage industry or the "domestic system", it concerned a great many so that being a worker in the industry needed no special mention in records. The system operated by the capital of the clothiers who put out several stages of the process to workers near the towns; the most famous of such clothiers was Peter Blundell, whose wealth founded his school in Tiverton, and a man like James Maynard,

"Clothier and Serge Maker" of Honiton, who was estimated to employ at least one thousand workers in 1752. The clothier bought wool from, say, the pastures of the Abbey lands, then took it round the villages so that the wool could be carded and combed, spun by spinsters and woven by men on the looms they had or rented from him; the cloth was then taken back to be finished by fulling, stretching, napping and presenting for sale, much of it in London, where the wool merchants had storage space at Devonshire Hall. Homes also made cloth for their own families. Devon wealth had been built up by, first, a rough and coarse cloth which was replaced by Kerseys in the late fifteenth century. A Kersey was a light cloth, made particularly in Cullompton, and it was in vogue for two hundred years. In its turn, it was replaced by a tougher and stronger cloth, serge, which had a flourishing export market in Europe until the whole trade declined rapidly before the competition of Norwich "stuffs" and, then, the advent of cotton - cheap, colourful and easily washed - the whole being hastened by the War of American Independence and the French Wars of 1793-1815. The collapse of the woollen industry was another cause for concern in Dunkeswell as it removed some vital extra income from many families.

Honiton Lace was an industry which required workers; in 1698, there were 1,341 employed in the town and 2,400 in 1800, with more in the surrounding villages. The flourishing industry was mainly for the nimble fingers of women and children but some men worked at it as well, after their main day's work. It gave work for Dunkeswell people, although Dr.John Yallop's study of the industry has shown it was not on the scale of surrounding villages. His breakdown of the 1698 figures was blank for Dunkeswell but revealed surprisingly high figures elsewhere; there were 215 workers in Luppitt, some 31% of its population, 118 (13%) in Broadhembury and Upottery (44%), 65 (25%) in Combe Raleigh and 64 (73%) in Monkton. Honiton Lace workers were specifically mentioned in the Census records; there were two in Dunkeswell in 1861, at Knapp Cottage and Richards' Cottage, 56 year old Mary Tolman from Precious Court in 1871 and one from a cottage near the Rectory in 1881. The industry declined in the nineteenth century, due to simpler materials being fashionable for dress designers, the various Education Acts removing cheap child labour and the impact of machinery, as at John Heathcoat's 1815 factory in Tiverton, employing 1,500 hands. The decay of lace was yet another blow, especially at a time of declining agricultural prosperity.

Census records show that Dunkeswell was a very self-contained village in the nineteenth century, able to offer the basics for work and living and being near enough to markets for other things. Some goods were delivered by

The Smithy, from an early C20th postcard

The Old Forge, today

Rosemary Cottage being re-thatched
by Master Thatcher Trevor Berry (on right) and Gary Lee

The Royal Oak, another example of the same thatcher's art

pony and trap, even in this century, and there are memories of a Mr.Singh, uninhibitedly called "the Black Chap", who came round selling clothes from suitcases, and of an oil and hardware van coming up from Honiton. There was a series of blacksmiths, both at Knapp and in the main village, where the Old Forge still is; in 1861, there were five working smiths. Thomas and James Cox were the Knapp smiths in the second half of the last century and the last working smith in Dunkeswell was George Lane. He and his family were rather cramped for living accommodation as the Smithy, in the 1923 sale details, contained not only the actual blacksmith's shop (a nineteenth century extension on the South side) but also a shoeing shed, stables, a cartshed and a piggery, with its garden backing on to the mill leat.Dunkeswell had carpenters and wheelwrights and there is still Carpenter's Cottage, opposite the Forge. Carpenters, such as James Parsons, lived at Knapp and others, like John Batten, worked in the workshop by the present Post Office in Dunkeswell village. The last carpenter at the Cottage, Mr.Lane, made coffins at £5 each while James Parsons doubled up as a wheelwright, to be succeeded by George Clode.

A thatcher was generally available, although he may have worked as a farmer as well, as happened at Knapp, and the thatcher at Wellsteps in 1881 was only a part-timer. Clarence Procter combined well digging with thatching and went on to run the "Royal Oak" in 1937. By repute, there was one thatcher who used to rouse his small son at 4.00 in the morning, to help him in his work; he got him used to working at a height by actually strapping him to the thatched roof on which he was working ! Smiths may have gone from the Parish but there are carpenters still at Little Musgrove and a resident thatcher in Tencery Orchard, although he lives in a slate roofed house. Well-diggers were available to exploit the water supply and wells were many in the Parish; there were, for example, two by Connetts. Sawpits, where one unfortunate always had to stand below the timber being sawn and receive all the dust and bits in his face, were situated at Knapp, Slade and Bowerhayes; there were claypits near Park Farm and Abbey Mill, a sandpit at Sheldon Grange and marlpits on the southern edge of the Parish. Marl, a mixture of clay, sand and lime, was widely used to fertilise the fields. Part of the main road to Honiton is Limers Lane, running through Limers Cross. Flints may have been useful in the very earliest days of settlement and, later, as a building material, but they had to be picked off the fields regularly and dumped, some to be used on the roads. Bark was another commodity for which there was some demand and it was gathered for the nearby tanneries, as at Payhembury and Colyton.

The village was well supplied with shoemakers or cordwainers, a name derived from the time when they worked with Cordovan, a fine grained leather from Spain. There were butchers, several carters and carriers, some dressmakers and milliners, a grocer or two, masons and tailors and a saddler and harness maker; in 1881, there was even a Staymaker at the Abbey. The last shops in the main village were at Wellsteps and the Post Office. Wellsteps was in the charge of a Mrs.Francis Ellen Wynne, described by those who knew her as "a little old lady in black who seemed to sell everything, in the room beside the front door". Later, Des and Eileen Marks took over that shop but it and the shop side of the Post Office both closed and have now been replaced by Highfield Stores, which stands in the middle of the new building.

To cater for them all, there was the "Royal Oak", the first reference to it being in 1753, when Richard Marshall and James Selway were licensed by the Quarter Sessions to carry on trade there. In 1755, the Parochial Returns had expressed surprise that the Dunkeswell Abbey Gatehouse had been turned into a public house, almost as much surprise as that voiced by the Devon & Exeter Gazette in 1923, when it learnt that the Gatehouse had been sold to a labourer ! A few years later, the Rev.John Swete was grieved that there was "not a pothouse in the parish", although he must have ridden by the "Royal Oak" on his way to Wolford Lodge. Edward Willie was named as a "beer seller" in 1850, then elevated to Victualler in 1857. Francis Richards held the licence for nearly the last thirty years of the last century and the early years of this century. In 1918, George Hornsey was conscripted into the army, leaving his wife in charge of the pub; it was for her that the Parish Council requested extra Police supervision over the foreign labourers in the village. Later licensees were Henry Middleton, James Elton, who was supplied with beer in 1928 from the Dorsetshire Brewing Co.Ltd., of Sherborne, Charles King, Clarence Procter, Robin Pike, Pat Flynn, Peter Cairns and Maria Howard. Trade and the building itself declined but the threat of closure was averted in 1973 and the "Royal Oak" stayed at the heart of the village. Another minor threat to its livelihood appeared in 1991, when Magistrates gave a licence for a public house which had not even been built. There was a remarkable comment on the success of the planners and builders when, at the Licensing Session, one of the Westward Developments directors, Shirley Wallace, stated that a public house was needed at Highfield because "the estate was divorced from the village, which had its own pub!"

Parts of the "Royal Oak" date from the sixteenth century but there have been many additions to it since then, such as the Coach House, and its present thatch; it stands just off the main road through the village and slightly above it. It is said that it was from that slight elevation that the USN personnel of the Second War used to wave their beer glasses and shout at the small parties of Prisoners of War who were being marched through the village on their way to work on the land. The various souvenirs left by the Americans, such as a collection of mess tins, have long vanished but what a good trade there was in those three years of so many at the USN base. USN officers were a bit wary of the "Royal Oak" when they believed that extra high alcohol content liquor was being sold there; in fact, the "Torpedo Juice" was 100% aircraft anti-icing fluid strained through bread crusts and very much a USN brew.

More recently, there has been the development of Fishponds House, outside the village itself; parts of it date from the thirteenth century, when it was a small house or cottage, but now it has been considerably enlarged to become a restaurant and a holiday centre. Keith and Kay Farmer are the fourth generation of the family which has lived at Fishponds House since 1895. Its name came from the ponds which were created to give a supply of fish. The Abbey itself had two large fishponds, very close at hand and clearly visible today; although both are dry, the retaining banks remain and the water supply, flowing from near Slade Farm via Stentwood, has simply been diverted to one side of the ponds. Those ponds should have been sufficient suppliers of fresh fish to the monks and the lay brothers at the Abbey; the Fishponds supply would have been a reserve for the Granges and of value to the Dunkeswell villagers who eschewed meat on Fridays and during Lent.

Today's village has a changed pattern of trades and shops and a very different clientele for which to cater but it is surprising how many services are still provided by those living within the Parish for their fellows.

Chapter 11

The People

It is hard to give true figures for the population of Dunkeswell before the middle of the last century. Domesday Book listed Dunkeswell as a Manor of at least eleven families of freemen and several slaves under their lord; after that, there was no accurate or comprehensive enumeration of the people until the second half of the nineteenth century. There were some rather haphazard reckonings and, even in the first few census takings, there was a strong opposition in England to being counted. Some believed it was morally wrong for anyone to count God's people and some opposed it because they were ignorant, illiterate or mentally retarded or some because a count might reveal criminal activities. The main opposition was based on fears of taxation and military recruitment. The Poll Tax of 1381, for example, was a count of heads for taxation and it caused the Peasants' Revolt in the South East of England and resentment elsewhere; later, strong opposition surfaced against the Hearth Tax of 1662, Land Tax of 1692, Window Tax of 1696, Male Servants Tax of 1777, Racehorse Tax of 1784, Female Servants Tax of 1785, Income Tax of 1799 and, even, against Mrs.Thatcher's "Poll Tax". The connection between enumeration and military and naval service was an old one, dating from William I's reign and feudal levies and going through to conscription in the two World Wars.

There are not many pre-nineteenth century records for Dunkeswell, nor are they consistently spread over the centuries, but what there are are valuable. The Devonshire Lay Subsidy of 1332 showed that there were 11 payers in the Parish. The County Taxation Returns of 1334 listed Olde Donkeswill as contributing £1.0.0, compared with the £2.10.0 from Hemyock and the 13/4 from Combe Raleigh. There was the Subsidy Roll of 1524/5 for "olde Dunckeswell Parish", when the ambitious Cardinal Thomas Wolsey was trying to raise money for the Henry VIII's war against France and other projects. The Subsidy's unpopularity and its lack of success both helped to ensure the Cardinal's fall in 1528. Dunkeswell had to find £1.0.8 in 1524, shared among 18 payers, and another 19/8 in 1525, from only 15 payers. The Subsidy was assessed at Michaelmas, when the harvest was in, on three classes - those who owned enough land, those who had goods to a certain value and those who depended upon their wages. Dunkeswell payers were in the bottom two groups: Land none; Goods 8 paid in 1524 and 1525; Wages 10 in 1524, 7 in 1525. The figures give some idea of the number of tax paying households but not of the non-payers. When Henry's war against Scotland needed money, he imposed another tax in 1544, demanding £2.10.0 from Dunkeswell, from 28 payers; the highest rated were Richard Vycary (property valued at £22), John Phillip Senior (£20) and John Phillip Junior (£19). In Devon, 345 paid the tax in Plymouth, 79 in Luppitt, 48 in Hemyock and 11 in Sheldon.

There were later surveys not made for taxation purposes, such as the 1569 Devon Muster Roll, which gave an estimated population of some 60 to 80 people. Next came another taxation record, the 1581 Subsidy for Dunckeswell Parish, when all with goods to the value of £3 or land worth £1 a year in rents were classified between G1 and G40 or L1 and L40, in ascending value. Winifred Buller appeared at the top of the list, in G15, and another widow, Joan Phillippe, came next, in G7. Roger Jeninge led the men, in G5, with Thomas Ley, William Galley and Thomas Cottell in the only and lowest Land category, L1. In all, there were 7 G and 3 L names, indicating little change in population from 1569. Had names been missing from the list, the Commissioners, Sir Gawin Carewe and Sir Robert Denis, and their Collector, John Eveleigh of Ottery St.Mary, would have taken action.

The next Parish record was that of the 1641 Oath of Protestation, to be taken by all men aged 18 and over, in those tense days before the outbreak of the Civil War. The fact that there were 86 names on the list would indicate a rise in the population since 1581, although the signatories were not merely those who owned property or goods. With women and children, the population must have been in the region of 250. Incidentally, the document illustrates the difficulties of genealogists; there were two Humphrey Coumbes, Richard Coxs and John Prowses and three John Rawes on the roll.

The numbers must have remained fairly steady, for some years, for the 1674 Hearth Tax return for Dunkshill Parish numbered 83; they

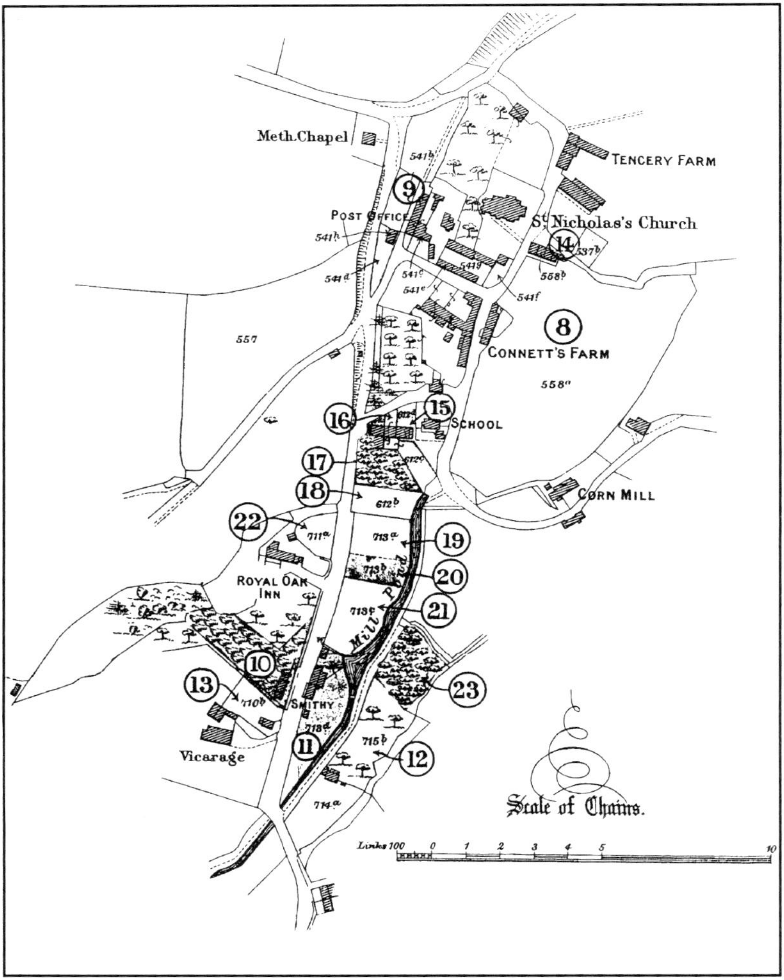

MAP 3: The Old Village in 1923,
from the Wolford Lodge Estate Sale Catalogue

were occupiers rather than owners of dwellings and they included the delightful names of Fairy House and Charity Pike. In 1817, as has been seen, the Dunkeswell Militia Return listed 72 men between the ages of 18 and 45; with women, children and older men, Dunkeswell must have had some 350 plus inhabitants. John Bailey's reminiscences of Dunkeswell life seem to bear out that there was a rapidly growing population. He wrote that in 1802 Dunkeswell village had six old houses and a small church, with seating for 40 people; the energetic and benevolent activities of the Simcoe family meant that, by 1850, there were at least 30 houses and seating for 1,000 in the Dunkeswell, Abbey and Luppitt churches.

The National Census was introduced in 1801 by John Rickman, who had unashamedly urged the "general enumeration of the people" for taxation purposes when Britain was heavily engaged in the long wars against France. He set up the Census Office and conducted the first four Censuses, 1801, 1811, 1821 and 1831, all of which were merely interested in numbers and names and occupations. So was the 1841 Census but a change came in 1851, when much more detail was required but not always given. The Census records for Dunkeswell for 1841 to 1891 inclusive are in the Record Office in Exeter and can be read there; later Census records cannot be seen until after a hundred years as they might well contain details of persons still living. Some of the Dunkeswell records are not as clear as one would wish; enumerators were not always highly literate, numerate or accurate and there were errors in transcribing the rough draft for the Census Office, when totals altered, houses became confused and age and sex details were muddled. That was especially true of the 1841 Census, when entries were not very clear or detailed, few house names and occupations were given, with age figures hard to read; in 1851, two pages were duplicated and pushed up the final figures; in 1881, many house names are indecipherable. From 1841 to 1891, the enumerators were Thomas Salway (4 times), Edward Salway, James Coles (2), Samuel Mark Junior, Samuel Maites and Samuel Kittow.

There was a steady rise in the population of the Parish before 1800, for the 1801 and 1811 figures recorded nearly 400 inhabitants, in line with the Militia Return of 1817 of 72 candidates for military service. Before 1851, the Census apparently indicates a falling population in Dunkeswell, while the population of Britain as a whole was rising rapidly. There was a local increase in 1860, then a gradual decline and evening out until the 1980s, when the new building programme boosted numbers to nearly 1,300 living in the Parish at the end of 1993.

Population figures for Dunkeswell Parish, from Census and local Directory sources:

1801	390	1861	490	1931	285
1811	390	1871	415	1951	240
1821	350	1881	390	1961	285
1831	300	1891	350	1971	285
1841	240	1901	290	1981	285
1851	260	1921	300	1991	1,300

The decline after 1861 marked an agricultural slump, one in common with the rest of Britain. More machinery meant fewer farm labourers were needed and foreign competition, especially from the great grain growers of the USA and Canada and the exporters of meat from the USA, Australia and New Zealand, brought concern for producers. The conversion of arable to pasture also lessened the demand for labour and, as labour was plentiful, so wages dropped. Several desperate men and their families must have used the means of greater mobility to escape into towns and industry, seeing little future on the land.

In Dunkeswell, records of baptisms, marriages and burials exist only from the second half of the eighteenth century, a frustrating state of affairs but not an unusual one. Clergy were often lax about keeping such records and many that were made were either destroyed through careless storing - a damp vestry or chest was not a good repository - or lost in some other way. Governments repeatedly urged that records be kept well. Thomas Cromwell, for example, in 1538, issued a Mandate about secure storing of records in coffers with two locks, with one key for the Parson and one for the Churchwardens. An Act of 1598 ordered registers to be on good parchment and up to date from 1558. The Civil War disrupted such efforts, especially when Puritan zeal destroyed Anglican registers, until Charles II ordered the recording to be put back into the hands of the clergy.

What ecclesiastical records we have, however, help to give some idea of population changes. Births can be gauged from the Registers of Christenings and Baptisms; Christenings officially became Baptisms in the new registers of 1813, ordered by George Rose's Act of 1812. The Registers start in 1750 for St.Nicholas's Church and in 1842 for the Church at the Abbey and numbers are slightly distorted because of the new Ecclesiastical Parish created for Holy Trinity Church in 1842, with bits taken from Dunkeswell itself, Clayhidon and Hemyock until 1929. The figures can also not truly reflect the birth rate as there were the occasional Baptisms for whole families, such as the five Brooms in 1845, at Holy Trinity, and the three Irish children in 1901. As time went on, too, it was no longer necessary for all children to be baptised or to be baptised in the Church of England and baptismal numbers fell off in this century.

Between 1750 and 1991, 2,160 were baptised in the Parish and they were almost entirely children; adult baptism was very rare. Many were baptised on Christmas Day and a few at Easter, to lend that extra sanctity to the occasion, and they were recorded as legitimate or illegitimate children. The breakdown of figures is:

						Average p.a.
1750 - 1799	=	467	in	50	years	9.34
1800 - 1899	=	1,228	in	100	years	12.28
1900 - 1991	=	465	in	92	years	5.05

One rather delightful entry in the Register for 1901, either through carelessness or a spelling failure, was that recording the baptism of Piggie Primrose.

At the other end of life, burial records speak for themselves. Burials were restricted to the two churchyards; although the Methodists were allowed burials in the Chapel grounds, the earliest grave stone dates from 1906, commemorating Mary Ann Drawer. Again, the increase in cremation affected the usefulness of the records as far as they represent the death rate. St.Nicholas's Burial Registers date from 1760, Holy Trinity's from 1842. Except for the odd comments, as in 1806 when General Simcoe was "universally lamented", they are straightforward lists of burials. The figures show:

						Average p.a.
1760 - 1799	=	192	in	40	years	4.8
1800 - 1899	=	693	in	100	years	6.93
1900 - 1991	=	323	in	92	years	3.5

Between 1760 and 1899, there were 1,608 Baptisms and only 885 burials.

The Marriage Registers start in 1754, a direct result of Hardwicke's Marriage Act of that year; it decreed that clandestine marriages had to end, banns had to be called and no marriages could be performed except by a clergyman of the Church of England, although Jews and Quakers were excluded. (Registry Office and Nonconformist Chapel marriages were allowed in 1836). Marriages had to be strictly recorded but there were surprisingly few in the Parish, including Holy Trinity. The figures show:

						Average p.a.
1754 - 1799	=	94	in	46	years	2.04
1800 - 1899	=	296	in	100	years	2.96
1900 - 1991	=	186	in	92	years	2.02

More useful for the social historian are the Registers of Banns, as required by the Marriage Act of 1823. The Registers for Dunkeswell start in 1824 and, covering much of the nineteenth century, they show the locality pattern of marriages of Dunkeswell people by giving the Parishes of intended bride and groom. "Intended" because not all banns actually resulted in marriages; in 1857, the parson recorded reading the Banns, as required by law, and added, "John Trimlett and Mary Richards. These parties were not married. The man went away and would not marry the young woman, as I was informed by her parents." Perhaps John Trimlett was not the only groom who had second thoughts. The only other comment in the Register was in the following year: "James Cox and Susan Richards (of Mary's family ?) married by me at Wolford Chapel, licensed by the Bishop during period of Parish Church being rebuilt."

Between 1824 and 1922, the Banns of Marriage for 276 couples were read in St.Nicholas's, at time of Service. Of those couples, 151 had both partners resident in Dunkeswell Parish and 125 concerned a bride or groom from another Parish. Closer examination shows that the area in which Dunkeswell people married was really a very small one of concerned neighbouring or nearby Parishes. Awliscombe and Hemyock head the list, with 12 mentions in the Banns; then comes Dunkeswell Abbey, with 10, during the years when it was separated from Old Dunkeswell. Honiton had 8, Upottery 7, Broadhembury and Luppitt 6 each, Sheldon 5 and Offwell 4. Other nearby Parishes were Blackborough, Buckland St.Mary, Churchstanton, Clayhidon, Culmstock, Kilmington, Membury, Sidbury and Wellington, all with 2; Cullompton, Culmstock, Exeter, Feniton, Halberton, Monkton, Northleigh, Nynehead, Otterton (Devon) and Otterton (Somerset), Ottery St.Mary, Payhembury, Pitminster, Taunton, Thorne St.Margaret, Uffculme and Uploman with a single mention. Further away were Paddington (2) and Basingstoke, Brackenford, Bridgwater, Chard, Chopham (sic)(Surrey), Islington, Kensington, Kentish Town, Newport (Mon.), Shroton (Dorset), Tollard Royal (Wilts), Torquay and Willesden, mentioned once each.

There are rather happy connotations on the 1839 page, when the Banns were read for a brother and sister, Mary Honniball of Hemyock to marry Thomas Webber of Dunkeswell and John Honniball to marry Mary Derham of Dunkeswell; in 1845, it was the turn of Henry Honniball of Hemyock to marry a Dunkeswell girl.

That there was a certain amount of movement round the country is demonstrated by the fact that some of those named in the Banns are designated as Sojourners or temporarily Residing in the Parish. Among the Sojourners, or temporary stayers, were Elizabeth Owen, in 1828, William Grabham and Richard Leman, 1832, James Browning, 1833, James Pitt, 1834, John Smith, 1835, and another eleven men and women up to 1848. In 1842, John Woodman and Mary Ashford are listed as Residing, as are another three up to 1853; Sojourner and Residing seem to be synonymous terms. Perhaps they were some of those itinerant workers who boosted the labour force in time of haymaking and harvest.

That there was movement into and out of the Parish is also shown in the Census records, even if that movement was mainly within the County and from neighbouring Parishes. In 1851, 109 claimed to have been born in Dunkeswell, 136 in other places in Devon and only 14 elsewhere, 5 of those coming from Somerset. The categories remained much the same in 1861 - Dunkeswell 224, Devon 222 and elsewhere 46, Somerset leading. 1871 showed more outsiders had arrived, with Dunkeswell 157, Devon 180 and elsewhere 91; in that year, the Vicarage contained people born in Devon, Somerset, Ireland and Cornwall, while Wolford Lodge boasted Devon, Somerset, Surrey,

Wiltshire, Cornwall and Hampshire and only one actually born in Dunkeswell. The pattern readjusted itself in 1881 (178/183/32) and 1891 (149/143/52).

It is often difficult to compare one Census record with another as houses were often named after their occupiers and so changed in time; examples of these are the Baileys' Cottage, the Clodes' Cottage, Davey's Cottage, Dimond's Cottage, Hill's Cottage, Richard's Cottage and Rowe's Cottage. Many houses had the same basic designation, simply The Abbey or The Village. "Farmer" was often a general term for anyone who worked on the land, as was "Scholar" for anyone at school, however unscholarly he or she may have been. Agricultural labourers also appeared as farm workers, farm servants, farm boys/girls, plough/plowboys and cattle boys. Several in the Censuses were listed as "Pauper", few as "Gentleman". Today, statistics are gathered for so many activities that life seems much more complex than it did for our ancestors; perhaps they felt they were freer individuals living in a less regulated society.

Chapter 12

The Poor and Public and Private Charity

Medieval families looked after and contained their own physically and mentally disabled and old as best they could, so there were very few who might have been a drain on community resources. It had always been so. People living near Dunkeswell Abbey were fortunate as they could rely on Cistercian generosity from the early thirteenth century onwards. The monks, as part of their Rule, devoted time and money to relieving the poor, either with food and simple clothing in the Abbey or by going to those in need. Charity was dispensed from the Almonry which stood near the main Gatehouse and the ideal of service to the poor was enacted every Thursday, when the Almoner had to select certain people whose feet the monks washed. The Almoner also had the power to greet poor travellers and the discretion to give grants unobtrusively. Undoubtedly, some English monasteries lost their willingness to give to the poor and suffered rebukes from Bishops on Visitations or, more lethally, from the officers of the Vicar-General,

Ruins of the Abbey Gateway, where the poor came for charity

Thomas Cromwell, in 1535/36. There do not seem to have been such direct charges against the Abbey, that it had ignored charitable works, but there may have been a decline in commitment which provoked indifference to the poor. Once the Abbey had been dissolved in 1539, however, the poor were left largely to their own devices and some may have joined the bands of beggars who roamed Tudor England, looking for work and food and causing fear; "Hark ! Hark ! The dogs do bark, The beggars are coming to town...".

The nineteenth century Census records show that Dunkeswell people still looked after their own; between 1841 and 1891, 18 paupers are recorded as living in the village, in households. The average number of people per dwelling was 6 in 1841 and 1851, going down to 5 in 1861 and 1871 and to 4½ in 1881 and 1891. There were, obviously, family units; Hooked Rise had 6 adults and 6 children in 1841, for example; four Abbey cottages had families of 8, 6, 7 and 9 in 1851 and Ball Cottage contained 5 adults; in 1861, Knap House had 4 adults and 4 children and Ashfords Cottage had 5 adults and 2 children; two village cottages had 6 and 4 adults in them, with 2 and 3 children in 1871; Beancroft, at the Abbey, had 5 adults and 3 children in 1881 and the Blacksmith's Shop contained 5 adults in 1891 but no children were listed. It was accepted that, as long as they possibly could, families rallied round the older members; as society became more mobile and children moved away to work, in the twentieth century, then the pattern of home care altered. That would have been especially so in time of agricultural decline.

The poor were sustained by a mixture of central government legislation and local charity. When unemployment became a real problem in the sixteenth century, the Tudors were forced to act, in two ways; they decreed there should be help for the deserving and impotent poor and harsh action against "sturdy rogues and vagabonds" who would rather beg and roam than actively seek work. One of the Acts passed in the reign of Edward VI, 15471553, was so savage that JPs allowed it to fade away; they were not prepared to inflict slavery and death on beggars. In the end, the Elizabethan government consolidated measures in the great Poor Law Act of 1601. The impotent poor were to be helped by Overseers of the Poor, who would collect a weekly Poor Rate from all parishioners and provide shelter and light work. The

1693 action by Quarter Sessions against the Bywood Farm tenant showed that his Rate was 3½d. each week, a sum to be recovered by legal distraint if he continued his non-payment. The Overseers would then build a House of Correction for those who refused to work; if they resided in the Parish, they would be committed to the House. If they came from another Parish and were caught begging, they would be stripped naked from the waist upwards, women as well as men, whipped by the Constable at the tail of a cart "until their backs be bloody", put in the stocks for 24 hours and then sent out of the Parish to the Parish in which they had been born or in which they had been resident ; a Magistrate would sign a passport for each vagrant, allowing so much time to get home. That basis of the English Poor Law was supported in 1662, when Charles II's government passed an Act of Settlement. A person was said to have settlement in a Parish if he was born there, had moved there to take up an apprenticeship or had worked there for more than a year; a woman became settled in her husband's Parish. If a man wanted to move to another Parish, he had to have a certificate that the original Parish would accept him back if he ever fell on relief and the Constable could escort him over the Parish boundary. Each Parish would look after its own and raise a sufficient Poor Rate so to do. That there were many poor in Dunkeswell is clear from the 1674 Hearth Tax return, when 30 of the 61 listed were paupers.

It is not known how well the system worked in the Parish until the seventeenth century; then, a reading of the Quarter Session records shows that the Magistrates were very active in administering the law and there was inter-Parish hostility over certain vagrants. Each case presents the reader with a small, human drama. In 1683, Dunkeswell and Honiton Parishes squabbled over which should support Susanna Bull and her three children; the Magistrates ruled against Dunkeswell. The Magistrates in 1700 adjudged that Giles Norrington, his wife and two children, "poor persons", had gone to Dunkeswell when they should have been settled in Pitminster, in Somerset, and ordered that the Pitminster Overseers pay the Dunkeswell Overseers 13/4d "for their loss sustained in this case". In the same sessions, Dunkeswell had to pay the Combe Raleigh Overseers 13/4d., when Agnes Cop and Margaret, her daughter, had been bundled out of Dunkeswell although that had been their place of settlement. The Dunkeswell Churchwardens and Overseers got stung again in 1710, when they had to pay another 13/4d.

to their Luppitt colleagues over Isannah Moore, who should have been settled in Dunkeswell. Another single parent appeared in 1711, when Sarah Hake, widow, and daughters Sarah and Elizabeth were sent back to Uffculme, which paid 6/- compensation to Dunkeswell. A complex case confronted the Magistrates in 1713. Elizabeth Baker had worked for wages for two years in Dunkeswell, when unmarried and childless; she had then left and "intermarried with one William Flower in the City of Bath", and William's mother told Elizabeth he had been born in Wincanton, Somerset. Elizabeth then gave birth to her son, William, in Somerton, Somerset; her husband must have deserted her and she and her son moved to Upottery, where she had no right of settlement. In the end, the Magistrates agreed she and the nine month old William should return to Dunkeswell. So the list of cases went on and Dunkeswell won some. Edward Griffin was sent back to Ottery St.Mary in 1722 while Goyne Thorne, his wife, Mary, and sons Samuel and Goyne were removed back to Awliscombe in 1731; in 1739, Hemyock lost in the case of the Wood family and Uffculme lost in the case of the four Ridges. Littleham had to accept back two Sarah Mays, mother and daughter, in 1740; Culmstock took back William Stephens, Mary and their four children in 1742, and Awliscombe was found to be the real place of settlement of John and Betty Ford. Other cases were lost. William and Jane Ridgway and three sons had been accepted back by Hemyock in 1724; then the Magistrates found that the Ridgways actually owned land and had money in Dunkeswell, although they were "poor persons", so back to Dunkeswell they came, presumably without any money by that time. Later records continue to show that Dunkeswell and other Parishes regularly fought their way through Quarter Sessions and, on balance, landed up all square and having to continue to levy the disliked Poor Rate.

The Tudor Poor Law was administered by Parish officers, under the direction of Magistrates; the chief officers were the Churchwardens and the Overseers of the Poor, backed up by Assistant Overseers and Parish Constables. To be an Overseer was a thankless task, being unpaid and subject to laws which some wanted enforced strictly and others with more humanity. Overseers were appointed by the Magistrates and they had to collect the Poor Rate every week and use it to cope with the poor. The Parish appointed the Overseers and theirs was an office which lasted well into the nineteenth century, although the new, centralised

Poor Law was in force at that time. The Dunkeswell Overseers' duties were taken on by the Guardians of the Poor, in Honiton, and the Overseers became simply the assessors and collectors of the Poor Rate. On the whole, the nineteenth century Overseers were men of some substance and they took the duties turn and turn about. Vestry records name many of them - Thomas Bright, James Burrough, William Chinnick, Francis Clements, Henry Critchett, Charles Derham, James Dimond, Samuel Farrant, Henry Irish, Robert Payne, John Reeves, Roger Rosier, Edward Salway, Henry and Robert Smith, Henry Vincent, John and Samuel White and Samuel Wood and even a woman at the end of the century, Mrs.Anne Burrough. The office of Overseer was not abolished until 1925, by which time the powers were negligible. Over the years, they had been helped by Assistant Overseers. In 1907, for example, Thomas Dimond, of Abbey Mill Farm, was made an Assistant Overseer and, because he had to collect the Poor Rate and deal with sums of public money, he had to find two Sureties in the sum of £100; he found them in Mrs.Jane Dimond and Mr.R.F.Burrough, both listed as Farmers, while in the same year, Mr.Tom Rosewell, another Farmer, stood Surety for an Assistant Overseer at Awliscombe. In 1910, the Assistant Overseer was George Hornsey and his Sureties were R.Smith and F.Richards.

By the end of the eighteenth century, the Overseers tried to find employers who would give employment and, in return, be subsidised by the Parish. They also had to ensure that the Apprenticeship laws were upheld and deal with recalcitrant masters and apprentices. For example, Isannah Moore, already quoted as a cause of dispute between Dunkeswell and Luppitt in 1710, had come to grief before that, earlier in the year, when she was discharged from her apprenticeship with Thomas Tussler of Luppitt, (Gent), by order of the Quarter Sessions; Isannah had been bound to her master by the Dunkeswell Overseers of the Poor and the consent of two Magistrates and, probably, some financial inducement. Thomas appealed to the magistrates, "it appearing unto this Court that the said Isannah Moore is Great with child. This Court doth therefore think fit and order that the said Thomas Tussler is discharged from his said apprentice". Quarter Sessions of 1727 held that Benjamin Webber had been bound apprentice to Thomas Griffin of Dunkeswell but he was to be taken over by the new owner of the property, Thomas Marshall. An Indenture before Quarter

Sessions in 1771 confirmed that Betty Ashelford had been bound apprentice to William Ellis by the Dunkeswell Overseers. The unfortunate Isannah Moore had compounded poverty with child-bearing and all Parishes were wary of giving aid to pregnant women lest they should burden the Poor Rate with extra charges; many such women were bundled over Parish boundaries before they gave birth.

Parishes and Magistrates were determined that unmarried mothers should be dealt with and the putative fathers of bastard children pursued, named and made to pay maintenance; in 1681, "Mary Browne was lately delivered of a base male child within the Parish of Dunkeswell which hath been chargeable to the said Parish; it is ordered that she be committed to the House of Correction to be put to hard labour and confined for one year from this present Session." In 1690, the Quarter Sessions put out an order on Bartholomew Balfour of Dunkeswell, "adjudged the reputed father of a base male child born of the body of Jane Stamp, singlewoman, in the Parish aforesaid .... and doth adjudge the said Bartholomew Balfour to be the natural father of the said base male child and order that the said Bartholomew Balfour shall pay .... the sum of one shilling and sixpence weekly and every week until the said base child attain the age of seven years from the birth thereof." Bartholomew also had to pay arrears of maintenance and a surety of forty shillings to the Overseers. In 1732, an Act of Parliament made it mandatory for pregnant single women to declare the name of the father of the expected child, making it easier for Parish authorities to insist on financial support for any bastard children. In all, in Dunkeswell, there were relatively few bastardy orders and private arrangements were usually and openly made for the children to be baptised and reared. The Register of Baptisms in St.Nicholas's Church shows the scale of the problem. In 1764, three out of nine baptisms were of "base children"; others followed in 1771, 1774(2), 1786, 1790, 1794(3/15), 1795, 1798, 1799, 1800(2), 1801, and so on, regularly through the nineteenth century, the last record being in 1890. At Holy Trinity, with the Register beginning in 1842, nine had been baptised by 1913; the last record was as late as 1940. The most horrifying case, when poverty and illegitimacy came together, was in the 1860 Burial Register in St.Nicholas's and it brings a chill to the heart; one child, "illegitimate and unbaptised brought from another Parish and died suddenly. Coroner's Inquest held. Buried on the Coroner's Warrant without Church service, not being baptised, as certified." The Honiton Union Guardians complained in 1911 that too many girls under the age of 15 or 16 were admitted to the Workhouse in a state of pregnancy and the following year they urged six months detention for any woman who should give birth to more than two children in the Workhouse; obviously, pauper women used the Workhouse as a maternity ward.

The Industrial and Agricultural Revolutions of the late eighteenth century and early nineteenth and the prolonged war with France produced a break down in the Elizabethan Poor Law all over England. It was replaced by the Speenhamland System; under that, labourers who could not earn enough to feed their families were able to obtain supplementary money from the Poor Rate, based on the size of the family concerned. In many ways, it proved to be of more benefit to the employers who realised that, if they paid lower wages to their workers, then the Parish would make up the workers' money; workers realised that thrift, late marriages and small families would reduce their cash benefits, such as they were. For example, there were several men listed in the 1817 Militia Return for Dunkeswell as being Poor Men and so exempted; James Pike was one. A 32 year old labourer, he had six children under the age of 14 and his family must have been a drain on Parish resources and yet he was an employed man!

When the Revd.John Swete rode to Dunkeswell in 1794, he was far from impressed by what he saw of the dwellings and the people. He had been directed to "the city of Dunkeswell" by a small lad and he received a shock; "To my mortification, I found Dunkeswell had half a dozen most miserable hovels, among which rose a small chapel-looking church with a diminutive spire. From a poor meagre smith, whose anvil looked rusty for want of use, I had confirmation of the lad's intelligence and that the road to the Abbey was exceedingly bad, that I must return the same way and that there was not a pothouse in the parish." When he rode on to the Abbey, he flinched at what he found and recorded his feelings in strong words: "On alighting from my horse to explore further (at the Abbey), I was in an instant encircled by a little host of children and females, whose tattered garments and meagre looks betrayed a variety of wretchedness the sight brought full to my recollection the objects of penury I had seen in another place .... Is it not a singular circumstance that the Children of Want, as in its flourishing days, should hover round the Abbey ? The sallow beings wandering about the ruined walls seemed to one like the Spirits of the Dead hankering after the bodies which they once animated ...... but in no part of the Abbey could I perceive the least vestige of grandeur or elegance ...... all is deformity ... nothing but pictures of distress ..... its inhabitants were now sheltered from the inclemency of the seasons by sheds erected from its ruins ignorance and wretchedness now occupied the site." John Swete had travelled extensively in Devon, from 1792, and such a sight was new to him; he left the area in a troubled frame of mind, as well as being hungry and thirsty. The situation could not have been much better some fifty years later, when Mrs.Elizabeth Simcoe and her daughters wished to build a new church at the Abbey; the prospectus issued to raise funds appealed for help to bring a church to an area which was "spiritually destitute" and where the only help the farmers could give would be the conveyance of building materials, "for such is the poverty of the district that no assistance could be expected from the rent of seats (in the new church)."

Of course, it was the richer farmers and other employers who paid the spiralling Poor Rate until the Whig government of 1834 introduced the infamous Poor Law Amendment Act of 1834. It was chillingly simple; there was no longer to be "out relief" or the distribution of money to the poor. Those who could not find work and had no one to support them were made to go into the Honiton Workhouse, in Marlpits Lane; it was built, solidly, in 1836. It was called the Union Workhouse because it catered for a Union of 29 Parishes and it was run by the Board of Guardians of the Poor. Conditions for the hundred and twenty inmates were dictated by the policy of "lesser eligibility"; in other words, conditions in the Workhouse were to be worse than conditions for the poor outside, so that paupers would not be encouraged to apply for admission. Those poor of Dunkeswell who could no longer be supported in the village would walk or would be taken by cart to Honiton; there, families would be split, to stop the poor breeding, to meet again only at meals or in the Chapel, where they had separate areas in which to sit. Often their heads were shaved, to deter lice, they were washed and put into Workhouse clothing and made to work at menial tasks, such as stonebreaking, gardening and laundering. They got out only when they had assured jobs or homes to which to go and that was not very often. They were looked after by the Workhouse Master, who was directed by the Board to do it all at the least possible cost, although the Honiton Workhouse records show that many of the Guardians were men of compassion who regretted the Act's stringency. They did not always support their Master, however, as in January, 1902, when he felt "obliged to complain of the conduct of the Porter, attempting to kick one of the Inmates (an Imbecile), also being very impudent and abusive to me." The Board assessed the Porter's alleged offence as "of a very trivial nature".

It is not known how many Dunkeswell men, women and children were admitted to Honiton, as the Workhouse admission registers no longer exist, but some estimate comes from the amount that the Guardians allowed each Parish, for their poor costs. In 1892, the poor of Dunkeswell cost the Board £71 for the first half year, while the cost for Luppitt was £131; that covered those in the Workhouse and the small amount of "out relief" that was being allowed, again. The following year, Dunkeswell half-yearly costs were £53, compared with Sheldon's £23, Luppitt's £92 and Combe Raleigh's £40. After that, the costs varied little, Dunkeswell always being much lower than Luppitt; in 1913, half-yearly expenses for Dunkeswell were £98 and £207 for Luppitt.

For numbers, the St.Nicholas Parish Register recorded the burial of pauper bodies brought back from Honiton. The first came home in 1837, the last in 1944. In between, there were twenty other such burials and one is listed for Holy Trinity in 1900. The Board of Guardians regularly asked for tenders for supplying coffins for the dead paupers from each Parish. In 1892, R.Mansfield of Luppitt quoted the figures of "Under 8 years of age, 7/6; Under 16, 10/ and Over 16, 14/". Strangely, his figures for Dunkeswell coffins were significantly higher than those for his own Parish. In 1894, he had dropped his price for the smallest coffins to 7/. The contract for coffins stated that "Coffin contractors should supply breastplate and handles, screw down each coffin and place the body in the coffin"; the bodies were also to be packed in sawdust. After 1894, there were only irregular tenders for coffins for Dunkeswell, although coffins for Luppitt were offered in most years. In 1913, Messrs Richards and Sons, of Queen Street, Honiton, put in a tender for supplying Hearse and Horses for funerals at home Parish Churches; their charge for Dunkeswell was 8/-. A few months earlier, the Workhouse hearse had been condemned as rotten after it parted in two at a funeral.

The Guardians were still very anxious that each Parish should contribute towards its own poor. In 1907, the Guardians received a letter from the St.Thomas Union, Exeter, asking that Honiton Union "accept the chargeability of Alice Ann Lester, aged 42, and her children, aged 3 and 1, deserted, on the ground that they were settled in the Union by residence at Wolford from April, 1902, to September, 1905". The Honiton Board adjourned the matter for enquiries to be made. By the next meeting, the Clerk had to report "that there was no doubt that the settlement was at Dunkeswell"; the Board accepted the chargeability, asked the St.Thomas Union to look after her and agreed to pay 1/- a week for each child. Two months later, the Board paid 11d. for a supply of Cod Liver Oil for Alice. After that, the Board regularly agreed that she be maintained in Exeter; by 1909, the cost was 6/- a week. In 1910, the Tiverton Union reported that Sarah Melluish had returned from Kentisbeare to Dunkeswell and that her relief payment from Tiverton had been discontinued, it being passed on to Dunkeswell Overseers. The case must have been contested as, four months later, Tiverton agreed to pay the relief of 3/6 a week. In 1912, "the Plymouth Incorporation asked the Board to accept James Spurway on the ground that he was born at Dunkeswell on 21st May, 1848, and having left home at 18 had been all over the County on Public Works but never residing in any one Parish or Union for over two years". Again, Honiton Union accepted responsibility. The same year, the Honiton Board pursued a woman in Dunkeswell for the sum of £23 which she held on behalf of an old man "recently removed to the Devon Lunatic Asylum, to repay the costs of his removal and maintenance, etc."; she so argued her case that the Board put the maintenance charge on to the man's two sons in Wellington. The poor man did not live long and the Asylum reported his death to the Board three months later. Reports about Union cases in the Asylum, either of progress and discharge or death, were frequently made to the Honiton Board.

James Spurway, having lived an itinerant life, would have been the type to interest the Guardians, unfavourably. The Police complained to the Board of "the danger, nuisance and expense to the rates caused by the great number of tramps infesting Devonshire" in 1893 and the Board agreed that there had been a general increase in numbers. In 1907, the Board recorded that 42 per thousand were paupers and that Honiton Union had, "with one exception, the largest number of old persons in the District on relief". In the next year, the number of tramps in the Honiton area had been 780, compared with 702 in Axminster and 322 in Taunton. The Board tried to reduce the numbers by instituting definite tasks for tramps; in 1912, they had to pound 1 cwt. of soft flint through a ½ inch mesh before they could have accommodation for the night. The interests of the poor of Dunkeswell were looked after by the elected Guardians of the Poor; four long serving Guardians in the nineteenth century were George Barton, William Clements, Samuel White and Samuel Marks the Younger, of Fancy Farm. Samuel Marks ceased to hold office in 1892 but agreed to step in the following year, when no one else was willing to take on the job. In this century, one of the most notable was Edward Burrough; his death was recorded in the School Log Book and the Honiton Guardians sent condolences to the family, on its loss, in March, 1911.

In 1908, the Dunkeswell Guardian drew the attention of the Board to a case of neglect by the local Medical Officer, who had failed to visit a Dunkeswell man in need. The Relieving Officer had failed to check that a visit had been made and he was reprimanded, as was the Medical Officer. The Relieving Officer, a Mr.Shepherd, had mixed fortunes after that; he had an accident at work the next month and broke his arm in two places and he was also suspended for failing to keep his books properly. The Medical Officer in 1910, Dr.Keppel Reede, was the subject of comment by the Dunkeswell Guardian, on the grounds that he lived too far away to do his job properly in Dunkeswell and hardship was brought on the sick poor of the Parish; he resigned the following month and was replaced by Dr.Stevenson. Dr.Stevenson was more active and he reported to the Board that he had ordered meat for three people in Dunkeswell after serious illness.

Because Dunkeswell was off the main roads, it never featured as one of the special places where tramps could ask for sustenance as they went through the County. This shortlived Way Ticket System of 1912 allowed tramps to pick up ½lb. bread and 2 ozs.cheese by producing the necessary ticket at Bread Stations at Axminster, Cullompton, Stockland and Fairmile or Willand, Hemyock, Upottery and Churchinford, with others coming later. After less than three months, the under-use and abuse of the system led to all Bread Stations being abolished except for those at Awliscombe, Branscombe, Honiton, Luppitt and Yarcombe;

they, in turn, faded away gradually, and tramps returned to the Honiton Workhouse.

There were attempts to improve the life of the pauper inmates. In 1893, they had been taken to the Bostock, Wombwell and Bailey Circus and Christmas gifts were collected for them, most years; the Mayor or Mayoress of Honiton usually supplied a Christmas tree. They also enjoyed some form of New Year Concert and the children went to the pantomime in Exeter in 1906. Easter invariably saw hot cross buns, Easter eggs and toys taken to the Workhouse. After Harvest, food parcels were sent by local Churches; in 1907, Awliscombe and Broadhembury took their turn. On special occasions, such as the Coronation of George V in 1911, inmates received extra rations for a week; earlier, in 1893, the inmates had feasted on roast beef and vegetables, plum pudding and a pint of beer each, with the women and children having tea, bread and butter and currant cake for tea and the men having another pint of beer and bread and cheese, all for the wedding of the Duke of York. To raise the self-esteem of the inmates, the Board decreed in 1912 that they should no longer be called paupers. The Board did allow alcohol on special occasions, normally for the sick, and they accepted a tender in 1913 for Ale at 9d. a gallon, Port Wine at 3/ and Brandy at 6/6 a quart. Tobacco and snuff could also be prescribed for the sick. Electric lighting replaced gas in 1912, when the Honiton Electricity Supply Company's tender was accepted. The Guardians also established three sorts of visitors to the Workhouse. There were the normal, personal or professional visitors; then, there were the Ladies, usually connected with the Guardians, who could cast a feminine eye over living conditions; finally, the Workhouse had to be open to the Surprise Visit, when Guardians were allowed access without any prior notice. In 1908, for example, these visits led to 20 feather pillows being ordered for the Infirmary, new mattresses suggested and badly baked bread being discovered.

The Guardians tried to do their best for the children towards the end of the nineteenth century and into the twentieth. A Workhouse School was established and inspected regularly by HMIs; there was a check kept on the Schoolmistress, who was rebuked in 1892 for taking adult paupers for a walk and allowing them to misbehave themselves. Two years later, the children were sent for a better education to Honiton National School and the question arose about what they should wear.

After considering that for a couple of weeks, the Guardians ruled against a distinctive uniform, which would ticket the children as paupers, and stated that the clothing "should not be uniform in colour or material or distinctive in any way". Some children were boarded out with foster parents, as was Florence Kate Garrard, who went to a Dunkeswell family in 1907 at a shilling a week. She also received help towards clothing and Charles Oliver, her foster father, reminded the Guardians that he should have received 10 shillings at Midsummer and Michaelmas, for Florence's clothing; the Guardians allowed his claim for the Midsummer money but disallowed the Michaelmas payment as Florence had gone into domestic service by that date. The Board also considered offers of other help; in 1892, there was a scheme to send destitute girls to Canada, while another offer, from the Emigration Home for Destitute Girls, restricted emigration to Canada to Protestant children. In 1908, the Exeter Association for Friendless Girls offered help; there was no report of acceptance of such offers.

Eventually, a more enlightened approach to the poor brought about the closure of the Axminster Workhouse in 1932, when the inmates were sent to Honiton; Honiton Workhouse closed in 1949, under the new social legislation of the Labour Government, and the building itself was used for Honiton Hospital.

The forerunner of the Parish Council, the Vestry, tried to help the poor and needy or to see that they were helped. In 1852, a proposal was carried "To defray expenses of the emigration of poor persons having settlements in this Parish and being willing to emigrate", under the Poor Law Commissioners' Regulations. Robert Burrough Senior and Francis Clements, as Churchwardens, were directed to borrow £30 for that purpose, to be repaid by six equal instalments from the Rates for Poor Relief. Unfortunately, it was not recorded who emigrated or where they went. At the same meeting, it was resolved that John Newton, having no means of supporting himself, should be put to husbandry work. Perhaps Dunkeswell tried to push him back to Hemyock, from whence he had come; in 1855, the Parish Clerk was ordered to inform Hemyock that "the settlement of Job (sic) Newton is acknowledged to be in this Parish". He died shortly afterwards. In 1869, the Churchwardens were asked to ensure that all did pay the Poor Rate; if any refused or delayed, legal action was to be started. The Vestry took action in 1857 to recoup payments made on behalf of Edward Salway, who had been Parish Clerk and who was to die the following year. His wife had been committed to the Devon County Asylum in 1856 and he was told to pay six shillings a month to James Dimond, Overseer of the Poor, towards upkeep and arrears, with a warning of legal action if he failed to pay. As late as 1905, the Vestry, under Samuel Kittow's Chairmanship, agreed to summon W.Westcott for non-payment of the Poor Rate; as no later reference occurred to the matter, he must have settled what he owed.

If the official relief of the poor fell to Parish and Church authorities, there was still room for private charity and, as in other areas, state charity has always been supported by personal charity. Most of it went towards the two churches and the two schools and but it was still of indirect help to the needy. For much of the time, individual families supported little groups of people, especially on the farms, where labourers joined the farmer's family in the farmhouse, and it was to the richest family in the Parish that people looked, eventually to Wolford. There is little evidence that the Lords of the Manor who succeeded the Abbot after 1539 dispensed much charity but the Simcoe family had a strong feeling of responsibility for Parish welfare. "As for me and my house, we will serve the Lord"; the text from the Book of Joshua included service to the poor and the Parish often asked Wolford Lodge for help. It did not mean to say that the Simcoes could not be firm with the needy. In 1826, it was reported to Mrs.Elizabeth Simcoe that Levi Richards and other men from Dunkeswell were building a house on the Turbury; Mrs.Simcoe recorded that Levi was a bad man and that she had ordered the building to be taken down but she did allow him to build further away from the Lodge. In 1837, it was to Mrs.Simcoe that the Revd.Mr.Clarke reported that he had been watching nine men, two of whom seemed drunk, lolling against the churchyard wall after morning service one Sunday; they seem to have gone before any action was needed.

The people of the Parish had always had rights to use the Common Land. They had Common of Pasture, enabling them to graze their cattle on the Common Land, and Common of Turbary (Turbury), which allowed them to take furze and to dig turf for fuel. Some had the right of Stray, that is they could allow their cattle to stray on to Common Land and not have them rounded up or impounded. These rights were always written into Indentures concerning the Lordship of the Manor and when land was leased or sold. An Indenture of 1664, between John Dawe and

Nicholas Lyne, both husbandmen of Dunkeswell, looked back to an earlier sale of land in 1630, when the Manor and Premises were taken over from the City of London by Theophilus Marwood and Hanniball Rowe with "Right of Common of Pasturage Turbary and Tillage in and upon the Commons and Waste Lands of the said Manor of Dunkeswell". It was a blow, therefore, when new farming methods caused large landowners to take in areas of Common Land and deny their use to the people. General Simcoe was an enclosing landlord and in 1803 he was given the legal right to enclose certain areas of the Parish. He did this under a Private Act of Parliament entitled "An Act for dividing allotting and inclosing all the Commons and Waste Lands within the Parish and Manor of Dunkeswell in the County of Devon". Perhaps he did not, at the time, appreciate the hardship he was inflicting on the Parish or he may have felt that enclosure would give added employment. By 1818, however, when another Inclosure Award was made for Dunkeswell, Mrs.Elizabeth Simcoe made an Allotment for Turbary. Under that, three areas were set aside for those with Right of Common and "for the poor people residing within the said Parish of Dunkeswell, to dig or cut turf thereon for their own use". The areas were at West Hill (37 acres 1 rood 16 perches), Collard Hill (3 acres 2 roods 27 perches) and Cox's Hill (2 acres 2 roods). In 1905, a report to the Charity Commissioners stated, "The land is not at present put to any profitable purpose. No turf has been cut for more than 30 years and the sporting rights are not leased". But, the granting of Turbary must have helped take away some of the bitterness of the poor.

The Simcoes created other charities and did charitable works amongst the poor, especially their own tenants and workers. Generous in their day, the charity bequests dropped greatly in value and proceedings were taken to wind them up in 1993. Charlotte Simcoe's Charity, under her will of 1832, bequeathed "To the poor and support of the school at Dunkeswell £10 per annum". Each year, the Trustees were to determine how much should go to "the most deserving and necessitous inhabitants of the Parish" and then supply them with "clothes, bedding, fuel, medical or other aid in sickness, food or other articles in kind, or pecuniary aid in special cases"; anything over after the school bequest had been met was to be divided between the clothing club and "pensions of 6d. a week to the aged poor persons of the Parish". Eliza Simcoe's Charity, under her 1864 will, gave money towards

Church Terrace Cottage;
two of the original 3 cottages which had formed the Parish Poor House.

educational and missionary work, as well as "£5 to the poor of Dunkeswell, being distributed by the clergy and the possessor of Woolford". The Parish Magazine recorded in 1970 that no Christmas parcels had been distributed by the Charities, probably because the value of the investments had dropped so much.

A more unusual Charity was the one of 1873, whereby Captain J.K.Simcoe obtained from the Parish the three cottages by the Church (now Church Terrace Cottage) and exchanged them for the Parish Room (now part of Corner Cottage), to be used as a schoolroom. Church Terrace Cottage had possibly been made from a seventeenth century farmhouse; it had been used by the Parish as a Poor House until the new Workhouse was created in Honiton. Perhaps, its original use continued, in a modified form, up to 1873, when the Captain's wife, Mrs.Mary Simcoe, put in as tenants old and needy Wolford Estate workers and dependants. The three cottages each had a living kitchen and two small bedrooms, the three being served by two earth closets outside. When most of the Wolford Estate was sold in 1923, the cottages were occupied by Mrs.Dowell, Mrs.E.Sparks and W.Pulman.

It is interesting to note that the cottage nearest the Church was crumbling in a postcard view in 1920; when it finally collapsed, the rubble was left there, condemned by the Parish Council as a public danger in 1961, until a television programme about Dunkeswell in 1970 caused it to be carted away. Because of the high mortality rate amongst its aged occupants, the Poor House was known to the local children as "the Dead House".

White's Survey of Devon in 1850 listed other charities which must have been absorbed elsewhere, later. It recorded that Charles Ford had left 20/- in 1583 and Nicholas Lack 5/- in 1670, both bequests for the poor of the Parish. Peter Holway left £100 for the poor, with which the Parish bought a house and 10 acres of land, rented out at £10 a year. At some time, Nicholas Marke left £5 in Rent charges for apprenticing poor children. The Survey also stated that the poor received £4 each year from an original grant of £110 from Mary Waldron's Charity of Clayhidon.

In 1869, to "enable the careful manager to buy home comforts which could never be obtained out of weekly wages", Mrs.Mary Simcoe started the Wolford Lodge Clothing Club for the poor of the Parish, a blend of Victorian self-help and moralising. It was open from the first Thursday in November until the last Thursday in October and, at the end of the year, gave premiums of fourpence on every shilling saved by Dunkeswell Parish people and threepence for people in the Abbey District. Savers were exhorted to "take care of the pence and the pounds will take care of themselves" and admonished that parents with children who "from carelessness or neglect do not send them to School" could not be Club members. Mary Simcoe was an active doer of good in the Parish, as Elizabeth Simcoe had been before her, and insisted on regular Church attendance and moral behaviour amongst the poor.

A later Charity was that of the Dunkeswell Carnival, started in 1953 to restore a more active life to the village; it was most helpful in the rehanging and purchase of the Church bells. The great money raiser was the Carnival procession; in its early years, that was always led by a figure of Lord Brewer on horseback. It was restarted recently but then went into abeyance, again, as most of the village organisations were all busily fundraising for themselves and enjoying the sense of community achieved by the participants. The Carnival had looked back to the days of the Abbey, when 15th, 16th and 17th August had been set aside for the August Fair for trade and relaxation.

Some land was given to support the Churches, especially at the Abbey; possibly, some fields were set aside for the rent to go to good causes. In the 1841 Schedule of Titheable Land in Dunkeswell, there appear Poor 5 Acres at Southey Farm and Long, Higher and Lower Poorsfields at Byewood, probably referring to the nature of the ground but possibly referring to the needy, as did such fields in other parishes. In any event, the people of Dunkeswell knew only too well the hardships of life, especially in a settlement so dependent upon agriculture and its vagaries and uncertainties.

Chapter 13

Health and Mortality

Information about the health of our ancestors in Dunkeswell is haphazard, mainly because of lack of records but, also, because of the stolid acceptance of ill-health by those who never had the services of a doctor and did not realise what might have been wrong with them. They certainly treated themselves with herbal and other cures, passed down from generation to generation; in 1826, for example, Elizabeth Simcoe came to the rescue of one of the Wolford tenants, Mary Hill, and took her Red Onions for her gallstone trouble, although the outcome was not recorded. They also feared some illnesses, especially diptheria; in 1897, the Mistress of Dunkeswell Abbey School noted the poor attendance of her pupils and wrote in her logbook, "Parents are afraid to send their children, diptheria having broken out, since Ellen Carter died".

The villagers almost certainly resented being questioned by public officials. From 1851, the Census takers were empowered to ask questions about certain categories of people and they would then have been listed as cripples, deaf, dumb, blind, disabled, lunatic, imbecile or idiot, in the blunt manner of the nineteenth century. But, because the Census takers were humane and unwilling to cause distress by categorical labelling of their friends and neighbours, especially if the declaration of an infirmity might well have cost a much needed job, and because it was the norm for families to rally round the less fortunate members of their families, there were few admissions of infirmity. The Census of 1851 clearly shows how the young supported the old in their dwellings and the pattern is repeated in later years. In 1871, a few handicapped people were listed; a man in 2 Sandy Lane had been crippled for two years; in the family next door, at Browns Nap, one had been crippled for ten years and another suffered from fits. At 1 Budhams Cottages, a seventy-eight year old agricultural labourer admitted he had been crippled for fourteen years, but he was still working. In 1891, the last Census available for public scrutiny, one of the dairyman's family at Musgrove's Farm was classified as an Idiot, probably meaning just slow witted, and one at Percy had been blind for thirteen years.

From the early thirteenth century, some suffering was relieved by the monks at the Abbey. The Cistercian Infirmarer would have been prepared to look after his brother monks and local people, especially those who worked as lay servants at the Abbey, in his Infirmary on the NW side of the Cloister. There, he used baths, herbs from the physic garden and the regular bleeding of the monks, Abbot included, to keep them in good, physical shape; bloodletting removed the ill humours from the body. The Infirmarer was exhorted to be "affectionate and gentle" to his patients and to the old and infirm. Part of the monastic Rule was also to go out to the poor and needy in the surrounding area. It was in 1348, however, that the people of Dunkeswell were faced by the great destroyer, the Black Death, for which the monks had no remedy. The bubonic plague swept through England in that year; it could attack anywhere and kill within days, with 60 to 90% of those infected being certain to die. The sickness was called bubonic from the buboes or swellings which accompanied it; the swollen glands occurred mainly in the groin, occasionally in the armpit or on the neck, being about the size of an orange. The blackness came from subcutaneous haemorrhages and a blackness of the mind with a destroyed nervous system. If the buboes burst, the patient usually recovered; if not, he died from the excruciating pain of the boils within four or five days. The Black Death caused great fear throughout England and it was particularly bad in the West Country as it moved inland from the port of Melcombe Regis. The Exeter Diocese suffered greatly and it was thought the sickness did not completely leave the area until as late as 1357. Nearly half the Diocesan clergy died and the Abbey was confronted with losses amongst the brothers and in the parishes for which it was responsible; the priests at Awliscombe, Upottery, Luppitt, Combe Raleigh and Broadhembury all died, the one at Dunkeswell survived. The Abbey was hard put to it to bring in new clergy, even though the Bishop appointed 345 priests in the first nine months of 1349, the usual number being 36. Awliscombe was without a priest for some time. There were further plague years, especially in 1546/7, 1571, 1590 and 1604/5. The first of these later outbreaks was noted by the Muster Commissioners for Devon, who failed to complete all their records of fit and able men because "Plague reigned so fervently in the County"; a mild and muggy Summer and

Autumn had been an ideal breeding ground for the germs which were killed only by severe frosts in the January. Dunkeswell may have suffered at other times but there were small pockets where infection did not reach. The final outburst of plague was in 1665, originally in London but spread through England by goods and refugees from the capital; after 1666, there was no more plague but there were other diseases and illnesses.

Influenza tends to be regarded as a twentieth century illness but it was known much earlier, as in the fourteenth century when sufferers were thought to be under the influence of the stars; at the end of the fifteenth century, Devon people talked about "The Great Sweat", allegedly brought to Wales with the invading troops of Henry Tudor in his successful bid for the crown. The symptoms tally with those of 'flu and there were epidemics of it in Devon in 1508, 1517, 1528, 1551 and 1557/8. Unlike most other illnesses, early outbreaks attacked the upper classes more severely than others and gained the name, "Stop Gallant", as a result. Later, it was more general in its spread. The 1551 outbreak was centred round Uffculme, while the 1556/7 epidemic was a pan-European one; even in England, there had been widespread failure of the crops in a very wet 1555, while 1556 was classified as a famine year - "All the corn was choked and blasted. The harvest excessive wet and rainy." The epidemic caused high mortality rates throughout England for a full year, relieved then by a bumper harvest in 1557. Attacks of 'flu probably continued but concrete evidence appears much later. Dunkeswell and Dunkeswell Abbey School records show that much teaching time was lost because of 'flu. The Abbey School was closed for several days in December, 1893; in 1898, many were away with 'flu in January and the teacher fell ill with it in March, so the School had to close again. The Head recorded two "bad weeks" in January, 1902, another attack in January, 1905, and in February, 1908, the Managers had to close the School for two weeks - no pupils and no teacher. 1918 was the really bad time, however, when 'flu spread from central, war torn Europe and reached England in October; that winter, 150,000 died in England from a virulent strain of 'flu acting on a population weakened by the privations of the last years of the War. Surprisingly, there were no recorded 'flu deaths, as such, in the Parish; indeed, only four burials were listed for the years 1918 and 1919, below the average mortality rate. The children suffered, however; at Dunkeswell School, the Head noted that there were several cases of the prevailing 'flu on 17th October and on 21st the Managers closed the School for a week as so many were away; it was to stay closed until 11th November. At the Abbey, things were worse and that School shut for five weeks from 18th October, with the Head also ill. After that, 'flu became part and parcel of school and adult life.

Smallpox appears to have been mentioned only briefly in Dunkeswell records but there must have been a fear of it, for General Simcoe had his family vaccinated against it in 1799; it was a brave action and typical of the General, at a time when the idea that cowpox infection could help to ward off smallpox was so new and Edward Jenner's first vaccination had taken place only three years previously. The General had probably seen the cartoon which showed people looking like cattle after vaccination with cowpox serum and read about "the cruel despotic tyranny of forcing cowpox misery on the innocent babes - a gross violation of religion, morality, law and humanity". But one Wolford Lodge child had not been vaccinated at the time and that was the infant John Cornwall Simcoe, born in 1798; to the great regret and sorrow of the family, John died in a smallpox outbreak of 1799. That year, Dunkeswell buried seven but there was no record of any having been smallpox victims, other than the baby. It was not until 1853 that compulsory vaccination for all children within four months of birth was introduced.

There was another scare, in 1893, however, which would have concerned the Dunkeswell inmates of the Union Workhouse at Honiton; the Guardians of the Poor heard with dismay that a sick German tramp had been admitted for a night's shelter, was too ill to go on and smallpox had been diagnosed. He was put in the Infectious Hospital at the Workhouse and nursed back to health by one who had already had smallpox; the Workhouse doctor told the Guardians that he survived because he had been vaccinated in his youth. However, there was to be no easy escape for the Guardians; two months later, a tramping family, George Light, his wife and three children, came from Richmond, Surrey, via Axminster Workhouse, where they had made no mention of feeling ill. The father and daughter went down with smallpox in Honiton and the special nurse brought in by the Guardians declared she had "never seen worse cases". The mother and eldest son were re-vaccinated and the ten month old baby thought to be safe; Tramp Ward admissions were cancelled for two days and the Ward disinfected. After lying "in a hopeless condition" for ten days, George died; the daughter recovered and she and the others were discharged, to go on their way to another Workhouse. Harriet Pollard contracted the illness but mildly and was soon up and about and thorough disinfecting and fumigation of the Tramp Ward and the Infectious Hospital seem to have worked but the Guardians had been shaken by the events.

Typhoid fever, typhus, dysentery and cholera were other evils that spread especially through people suffering from poverty and malnutrition. Dysentery, or "the Bloody Flux", came to all areas in Devon in 1540, a year of the great drought from February until mid-September, when streams and wells dried up, cattle died and people suffered from lack of fresh drinking water. Typhus occurred as a reference in the Dunkeswell Burial Register for 1839; having recorded the burial of a 44 year old labourer, Samuel Harding, and his child, John, on 19th September, and that of Samuel's father, the 82 year old labourer Henry Harding, shortly afterwards, I.T.Mansell, the Curate, added, "The Typhus being prevalent". Typhus was known as a poor person's disease, being carried by lice, fleas, mites and ticks and affecting those unable to wash often. Patients suffered from headaches, fevers, jaw and joint pains, delirium and a rash. The coming of cheap soap and cheap cotton clothing helped to defeat it. Poor food and poor housing were other adverse factors and, in times of unemployment and low pay for labourers, malnutrition was not very far away; in June, 1919, for example, malnutrition was recorded in the case of three Dunkeswell Abbey School children, who also had scabies, and they were sent home.

Limited cleanliness and poor feeding often appeared in the same families and schools all over England recorded similar cases, so Dunkeswell was not unique; the Mistresses had to be scrupulous in their records and reports of absences through medical conditions helped to offset poor attendance figures. References to skin ailments were nothing new, either; in the great frost of 1739/40, it was recorded of Devon that "a nasty Itch was now universal amongst the lower kind of People", attributable to the lack of washing and non-changing of clothes. Later, the Headmistress of the Abbey School wrote in her Log on 3rd August, 1903, that two children had been sent home "suffering from that very offensive and contagious disease known as the 'Itch'".

On 8th September, 1914, one Abbey girl's hair was stated to be "alive with vermin" and she was not to return until clean; the poor girl was sent home again twelve days later as the condition had returned. In Dunkeswell School, similar cases were noted; in 1917, one boy was reported to the Medical Officer of Health and was away for twelve days and three more of one family were excluded for lack of cleanliness in 1922. As late as 1938, the District Nurse came to Dunkeswell School after reports of dirtiness of some pupils. Perhaps Dunkeswell was lucky to escape as lightly as it appears to have done. Local authorities tried to take some preventitive measures to ensure children were nourished and clean; from 1915, notes appear in the Abbey School books that the Nurse checked children's heads and bodies and began to weigh and measure them. In 1920, the Abbey Mistress ran into disputes with parents over the Medical Officer's edict that all girls should have their hair plaited and tied back. In 1927, the Abbey School began to have talks on basic health and hygiene. There were also more mentions of the School being scrubbed and cleaned thoroughly from 1928; inspections and cleaning were carried out at the same time at Dunkeswell School. In 1936, Dunkeswell parents met in the School and approved a scheme for providing a good and hot meal at lunchtime; the parents provided vegetables and milk and the School did the rest, on Tuesdays and Thursdays, at a charge of 1d. per meal. Malnutrition surfaced again in 1938 and the Doctor and Nurse spoke to parents about nutritional values. More worries came with the influx of wartime evacueees, when local people were disturbed by the eating habits of the children placed in their charge, their resistance to washing and many cases of bed-wetting; checks on "suspicious heads" were regularly carried out in Dunkeswell School and the Rectory Room. Cases of ringworm appeared every now and then and one or two had scabies; the sufferers did their best not to scratch but there was no quick cure.

Diptheria was a dreaded infection; again, there is reference to it in the Burial Register for the summer of 1881, when three of the Moore children died within days of each other; Clara was two, Walter nine and Frank eleven. The Abbey School Log and Admissions Registers record later outbreaks and reactions to them, although the Dunkeswell School Log has nothing. In 1893, there were no warnings, apart from two families keeping away their children in September, with ulcerated throats, and a general spread of what was diagnosed as 'flu early in

December. Then, there is the entry, "Arthur Spiller deceased; Complaint Diptheria". Arthur had entered the School at the age of three and was dead at five. The first Log entry for 1894 recorded "Eva Spiller is also dead, she died from the same complaint"; aged eight, she had entered in 1889. Both the children of William Spiller had, in fact died on the same day, 22nd December. The School closed for a few days, in face of the parental concern about the spread of diptheria; the concern was justified for on 10th February, 1894, the Mistress wrote, "Diptheria has broken out on the Madford side of the School and others in the district are suffering from ulcerated throats", including herself, so the School shut again. That outbreak cleared itself and another came in 1897. Ellen Carter of Hemyock had already died in January, aged eight, "from Cold, caught after recovering from the measles", cases of diptheria were reported on 1st February and James Carter died from it on 11th February. James was also from Hemyock and he had been at the Abbey School from 1891, when he had entered at the age of four. Other children were away ill but there were no more deaths, then. Another Abbey death came in 1911; the onset of diptheria had been noted on 28th October and, three days later, Emily Aplin, of Trickeys, had died from it, at the age of eight. The outbreak went on into 1912, when a prolonged bout of Mumps took its place. In 1938, renewed diptheria fears led to Dunkeswell children being inoculated in the School by the Medical Officer of Health and he came back in following years to check that all were covered by the inoculations

Apart from the usual coughs and colds, many other childish ailments were recorded; Mumps, Scarlet Fever, Chickenpox, Measles and Whooping Cough all spread rapidly and all disrupted the Schools' routine. One set of aggrieved parents must have been those of Minnie Pike, who had brought Whooping Cough home with her from hospital in 1913. Other occasional maladies were logged in the Schools - chilblains, ulcerated throats, rheumatism and illnesses of an unspecified nature. Fanny Clapp, of the Abbey School, was reported as being "very ill" in November, 1895; Ernest Eveleigh had the same entry the following year. The Abbey Mistress was lost for diagnosis in 1911 and could state only, "There is a general sickness among the children, comes on with a pain in the stomach and the eyes turn yellow". One boy had a heart condition and fainted in afternoon school one day in 1912, when "water was applied until he came round". The modern illness of stress was there, too, when the Dunkeswell Mistress was away for nearly the whole of November, 1923.

More serious were the attacks that caused children's deaths. William Sanders had been admitted to the Abbey School in 1887, at the age of five; at the age of ten he died after an illnes of four days, listed as "Brain Fever". On 29th July, 1915, "Little Frances Thomas died yesterday afternoon from a bad attack of croup." Croup was a virus infection which attacked the respiratory tracts of young children, not very common and not always fatal, but Frances Nellie Thomas, aged five and a half, of Middle Mackham, succumbed to it in her second year in school. On 24th February, 1911, Hilda Doble, of Madford, died of appendicitis. The twelve year old Elizabeth Broom, of the Dunkeswell Council Houses, died in Exeter Hospital in 1932 after what must have been a prolonged illness; her School had already received an Exemption from School certificate way back in 1929, granting her leave of absence for twelve months. Another death that affected the Abbey School was that of the baby daughter of the Vicar of Holy Trinity, W.P.Roberts. The birth of the little girl had been celebrated the year before and her Baptism marked by a tea party for the schoolchildren in the Vicarage Field; less than a year later, "several of the children attended the funeral of the Vicar's baby". The children at both Schools must have become accustomed to illness and death; reading the records gives an impression of grief and sympathy but also of an acceptance of events.

Children being children, there were always accidents logged, sometimes with the treatment given to the casualties. The Abbey School does not seem to have had as many minor accidents as Dunkeswell School, perhaps because of slightly smaller numbers. Abbey children might tend to fall into the water but the accidents that happened to them were all at home. In 1915, "Reggie Doble, aged three years, was kicked very badly in the head by a horse directly he returned home from school last Friday afternoon. He is in a critical state." Philip Pyle broke his arm in the hayfield in 1917. In 1918, Walter Kelland died, a week after an accident. Family accidents were also recorded; 1916 saw the death of a father in an agricultural accident and the injury to a boy's sister, who caught her hair in a Separator.

Dunkeswell School pupils were more rumbustious. Frederick Quick fell in the playground and hurt his thumb in 1918. Teachers have always disliked wet dinner times and horseplay occurred in the same year; "Reginald Driver accidentally caught Frank Evans's ankle round the iron standard of the desk causing a sprained ankle in wet dinner hour"; Frank was away for a week. The children might well have been surprised at the meticulous recording of their accidents; "Vera Canniford fell down when running down the road at 1.15. As her knee was badly cut a message was sent home and her mother fetched her at 2.20", on 14th May, 1928. Poor Beatrice Proctor was knocked down by a bicycle by the School and badly hurt in 1933 and, in 1936, bruised both her knees in a playground fall. Gordon Mountford must have hated the application of iodine and a bandage to his cut knee in February, 1936, especially as he had cut his hand the month before. The Mistress's hot fomentation would have been equally bad for the three pupils who fell down on gravel in March, 1936. Donald Stevens was another injury on the playground in 1938 - another hot fomentation to a cut knee. It was not a good year; Jean Evans cut her knee and Frank Canniford his top lip and knee in April, while Stanley Eveleigh's knee suffered after he had slipped in his hobnailed boots. To round off the year, Walter Eveleigh hit his head against a wall and Dr.Evans had to put a stitch in the wound. Leonard James Procter's gashed and three-stitched knee in 1941 was the last of the recorded Dunkeswell injuries.

The apparently gloomy picture of illness and accident was lightened by the longevity of some of the people of Dunkeswell. One or two of the earlier entries in the Burial Registers may be slightly suspect because many were born before the legal requirement of the 1836 Registration Act to register births, deaths and marriages and ages were sometimes based on hearsay or faulty memory. Even so, some good ages were recorded in the Registers which go back to 1793, although ages at death were not entered until 1813; in that year, one of the first entries was for Mary Webber, aged 100, who would have lived through the reigns of Anne and the first three Georges. Of the ten buried in that year, four had reached 50 years of age. Mary Acland died in 1823, at 96, Mary Ley at 97 in 1826 and Thomas Acland at 99 in 1827. Between 1843 and 1882, seven parishioners reached the mid-90s. There was then a gap until 1910 (Anne Clements 93) and 1927 (George Hornsey 94), reinforcing the theory that ages at death had not been quite accurate in earlier cases. Generally, the death rate was not as high as might have been expected and those who reached their teens usually lived on into old age.

The Registers also show the decrease in infant and child deaths as medical science improved and better food increased resistance to illness but Dunkeswell still lost many before the end of their first year, for one reason or another. In 1813, ten were buried and four of those were below one year old. In other years, infant mortality was also high; 3/5 burials in 1819, 3/6 in 1824, 3/7 in 1834, 4/9 in 1838, and so on. In September, 1836, two of the Hitchcock children died, John an infant and William aged four. Mark Moore, a butcher, and Mary, his wife, had their infant son baptised at home on 27th March, 1842, and he was buried on 3rd April. The Holy Trinity Register began in 1842; in 1844, all three burials there were those of infants and in 1890, 5/7 were infants. In the 86 years between 1813 and 1900, there were 505 recorded burials in Dunkeswell; 104 were infants, 54 were aged between one and ten, so the infant death rate was 20.6% of the total and the under ten death rate was 31.29%. The combined figures for Dunkeswell and the Abbey, between 1842 and 1900, show that infant deaths were 19.43% of the total and under ten deaths 29.8%. National infant mortality between 1850 and 1900 was 15.44%, so St.Nicholas's and Holy Trinity burials were slightly above the average.

The Schools did their best to keep an eye on pupils' health; details of medical inspections figure at the Abbey School from 1915, when a dentist and a nurse filled and extracted teeth, and, at Dunkeswell School from 1917, when pupils were weighed and measured, and visits by the Nurse, Medical Officer of Health and the Dentist became regular events, generally well received by pupils, especially when the Nurse and Father Christmas arrived together in Dunkeswell on 2nd December, 1935. Not all parents agreed to treatment actually being given, however, and the Dunkeswell Log recorded that things were much better in 1937 when only one set of parents objected to dental examination and treatment; by 1938, no parents objected. Eventually, oculists and psychologists visited from the 1930s onwards. In cases of anxiety, a Board of Education inspector might check the cleanliness and suitability of buildings, as in the Abbey School in 1895, when he reported that "the stone floor is very cold ... and the closets need more light and ventilation". A Sanitary Inspector might check and close a school, as happened at the Abbey School in 1911 over a five week period, until it had been cleaned and disinfected; another looked at the water supply in Dunkeswell in 1933, for some unspecified reason.

The Schools had to work under conditions which were not always of the best. A piped water supply did not reach Dunkeswell until the arrival of the Americans in 1943, mainly because of the natural supply through wells and springs, although the purity of that water could not always be guaranteed during times of drought or flooding or from farmyard pollution. The Cistercian monks at the Abbey had been most careful to discharge any effluence into the Madford River below the part of the river used for drinking and cooking purposes; other inhabitants might not have been so careful. There was a plan about 1911 to build a new classroom on to Dunkeswell School, so enabling the pupils to have better cloakroom accommodation as well; a ¾" galvanised pipe would be taken across the road to the public supply at the well, to feed water into two basins in the cloakroom, to encourage cleanliness. Mrs.Mary Simcoe, however, wrote from Wolford to the Rector, as it would have been on her land: "I do not feel disposed to have water carried from my new arrangement into the School. It seems to me quite simple to have a can full carried across as needed." Not a very encouraging reply but nothing could be done about it. In 1944, Alfred Le Marchant explained to the Parish Council plans for the water supply to the village; greeting the proposals with enthusiasm, the Council also hoped that electricity and a sewage scheme would arrive.

The School itself had, of course, earth closets and a primitive urinal and the main sewer did not come to Dunkeswell until 1970. In the great Wolford Estate sale of 1923, there are significant details in the sale catalogue. 37 dwellings were put up for sale; 26 of those had outside earth closets, the three parts of Church Terrace sharing two closets. Wolford Lodge had two water closets inside the house and two outside and Southayes had one inside. There was no mention of any facilities in eight of the dwellings. For water supplies, 21 of the dwellings had no mention; one had a pump from a spring, 12 used wells, presumably private ones, and 3 used the Village well. How the nineteenth century villagers would have marvelled at the present water and sewage systems and envied the luxury of water on tap. Some of those giving evidence in the Village Hall, recently, to a Women's Institute enquiry on conditions earlier in the century, vividly recalled the amount of time and energy they spent carrying water and the inconvenience of the little shed at the bottom of the garden, especially on a cold and wet night !

They also recalled the visits of the doctors. Some in the Parish received medical attention in Honiton surgery but most stayed in Dunkeswell. There was Dr.Sydney Huth, who had a practice at Culmstock, using the Dunkeswell Forge for consultations at 10.30 on Tuesdays and Saturdays. A regular branch surgery was opened soon after Dr.John Lysaght Griffin arrived at Hemyock in 1926, in his own practice. The villagers remembered his arrival at Corner Cottage. He would park his car in the road, so his own and other children who had come along for the drive could get down, and greet those who were waiting for him; some had walked or cycled a long way, including the carless owner of the Stopgap Garage on the A303. The waiting room in the summer was the grass verge and the area round Wellsteps and the consulting room the rather barren Parish Room, now the kitchen of Corner Cottage. Some of the medicine was kept in a cupboard there, several bottles of stock medicine for coughs and indigestion; the rest was brought by Doctor Griffin. If necessary, patients were recommended to Honiton Hospital. Dunkeswell surgeries were from 12.00 to 1.00 every Tuesday and Saturday. Dr.Griffin's children often accompanied him and recall how far their father had to drive to reach some patients. A family joke was that, when the good doctor arrived home after a busy day, he would be told there was an emergency call; on enquiring where, he would be told it was at Hookedrise Farm, to reach which he had to drive round fields rather than across, undoing and refastening gates as he went and making a long detour. During the last War, the doctor was allowed to drive to Dunkeswell round the perimeter track of the airfield via a slip lane by Slade Farm, except on the occasions when armed sentries turned him away because of some security scare or other.

Dr.Griffin was succeeded in 1948, when the N.H.S. came in, by Dr.Thomas Logan, recently graduated from Glasgow University; he had an interest in anaesthetics and became a consultant in Taunton, being replaced by Dr.John Griffin Junior, who had returned to Hemyock in 1958. The branch surgery was moved to the Post Office, Bankside Cottage, by arrangement with Mr.& Mrs.Vestey; patients waited on the verandah, there, and listened to the symptoms being described to the doctor by other patients, although Dr.Griffin recalls that he could not but overhear those waiting describing their own symptoms enthusiastically and loudly to fellow patients. Malcolm and Daphne Andrew allowed the Surgery to remain when they took over the Post Office but, eventually, it moved to the kitchen of the Village Hall, where there was cold running water and a substantial table on which were examined pregnant mothers and others before the table went back into the main Hall. The doctors in the 1930s were helped by Miss Cannon and Miss Carter, District Nurses based in Honiton but available to patients in Dunkeswell. In the end, most Dunkeswell patients attended the Hemyock Surgery of the Blackdown Practice until the building of the surgery at Highfield and the daily attendance of doctors there, backed by hospital facilities in Taunton and elsewhere.

Dunkeswell School, with the original Police House (badge above the door) and the Shop (sign above the window), from a 1920's postcard

Dunkeswell Abbey School, now a private house

Chapter 14

Schools

Dunkeswell was fortunate in its schooling, owing much to the Simcoe family and its concern with the welfare of the people in the Parish, especially the young. Robert Raikes had introduced the idea of Sunday Schools in 1780, in Gloucester, to take children off the streets, improve the moral, religious and educational standards of those children and prevent idleness breeding vandalism and mischief. For many of those city children, Sunday might well have been the only day of freedom they had, especially as factory life became all pervasive for the lower classes. Children in Dunkeswell worked hard, also, with long days on the farm, but they did not pose the problems of city children. However, in 1806, the Curate, Richard Pratt, opened a Sunday School in Dunkeswell, with the strong moral and financial support of Mrs.Elizabeth Simcoe. It is not recorded where the School met or for how long, although it had nearly 50 pupils in the 1851 Religious Census.

Main education came to the Parish in 1832, when an elementary school was created, known as the National School, after the National Society for the Education of the Poor in the Principles of the Established Church ! It was also called the Parish, Voluntary or Church School. Much of the drive to establish it came, again, from Wolford Lodge; the school was supported by the Simcoes, especially Charlotte Simcoe's Charity of £10 per annum, to be shared with the poor, and by "the children's pence". It met in the Parish Room, the extension at the rear of Corner Cottage, and began with the surprising number of 35 pupils, or "Scholars", as they appear in the Census. Little is known of the early years apart from references to teachers in local directories; in 1850, Thomas Kirby and Ann Gosling were named and Mrs.Sarah Salter in 1857, 1861, 1866 and 1870,being joined by daughter Sarah in 1861. They lived in Wellsteps, the cottage next to Corner Cottage.

In 1870, Forster's Education Act made it compulsory for Schools to be set up in Districts where insufficient elementary education was provided. The Dunkeswell authorities, the Vestry, considered what action should be taken and decided, in 1874, that no School Board was wanted, the education of Dunkeswell children should stay in Dunkeswell hands and that a committee be appointed to draw up action plans. On that committee were Captain John Kennaway Simcoe, R.N., the Rev.William Balmain, William Clements, Samuel White and Samuel Smith. The committee reported to the Vestry that the School should remain a voluntary one, financed by a rate and donations, prominent landowners should be asked to help, it was not feasible to alter the Parish Room and a new school should be built. Samuel Farrant, Samuel Marks and Henry Irish joined the School Committee, which asked for tenders and awarded the building contract to T.Granger & Sons, at a cost of £170. By the end of 1875, £76 had been subscribed towards the building and annual running expenses were estimated at £23. The site was given to the village by Captain Simcoe and the School opened in 1876, accommodating 64 children in the simple, plain building which is now the Village Hall.

Although the 1870 Act had made the provision of elementary education compulsory, it was not until 1880 that attendance was made compulsory to the age of 10, later to 11, 12, 14 and 15 (1944). Children might have to stay in school longer if they failed to notch up enough attendances or reach certain standards; the Abbey School Log noted in 1906 that a boy had left, "having obtained the Dunces' Certificate !"; later, they were Labour Certificates. It speaks well of Dunkeswell that so many children attended before attendance was compulsory and that parents were, generally, supportive, particularly when encouraged to be so by the Simcoes. The School was managed by the Vicar, the Churchwardens and four other people, resident in the Parish or within five miles of the Parish, being contributors to the School funds. The Admission Registers exist from 1911. They show that Arthur Merchant entered the School in 1911, aged 4; in the same year arrived three Walls from the Royal Oak and four Stevens from Mansells, while five Hounsells, of Lower Southey, arrived in 1912. Dorothy Burrough, of Southayes, aged 5 (Admission No.60, 1916), later became a Monitress at the Abbey School; four more Burroughs entered from Sheldon Grange in 1921 and another one from Southayes. The last to enter were Arthur James Clist (Percy Hill Cottage), Leslie George Gollop (Percy Farm), Bernard Thomas Morton (Little Tencery) and Robert John Pile (Park Farm).

The children at the Abbey were more fortunate than the main village children in that they had a purpose built school and house as early as 1847, directly founded and funded by Mrs.Elizabeth Simcoe and then supported by Eliza Simcoe's Charity or "Educational Foundation", of £5 per annum. There was a two room plan house at the back and the single storey schoolroom, all in the Tudor Gothic style, to which some alterations were made in 1873 and in this century, when the large window was added to the schoolroom. The School had high aims, for the Devon Directory of 1857 stated that the School "was privileged to take the sons of farmers and tradespeople", with room for 50 pupils under Thomas and Mary Hosegood. Before the Hosegoods was Ann Squires and after them Thomas and Eliza Moon. Admission Registers exist from 1879, when three girls and nine boys were admitted, including Elizabeth Honiball and four Dobles; six came from Hemyock and two had transferred from Dunkeswell. That it was very much a family school is shown by the 1884 admission of five Newberry children from Hemyock, aged between 3 and 8, five Carter children, also from Hemyock and aged between 4 and 9, in 1886, and five Irish (family, not nationality) children from Clayhidon in 1899, aged between 3 and 11. 1911 saw the admission of the rather splendidly named Artemas Cuthbert Radford, of Abbey Wood, and the 1927 entry of 11 children included two girls from Newcastle and two boys from London.

Both Schools gave a good education and the Simcoes continued to help, accepting state aid in 1891, when elementary education was made free, and the authority of Devon County Council in 1905 and supplying things like books and slates in 1890, maps in 1891, Drawing material in 1892 at the Abbey and books and coloured plasticine in Dunkeswell in 1918. They also gave prizes, over the years, including one for what might have been a dangerous hobby, the best collection of poisonous wild plants, in 1922.

Diocesan and Board of Education inspections took place regularly, with various comments. At the Abbey, the 1892 Inspectors reported that "instruction suffers from very irregular attendance" and the Managers were told to do better. Children tended to stay away with what their teachers regarded as very insufficient excuses; it was bad for the pupils themselves, bad for the gaining of grants based on good attendance figures and bad for teachers' career prospects. The teachers kept pointing out that attendance records should be discounted because of ill health and bad weather. The Logs record that children stayed away for haymaking in many years (Abbey, 1903, ".... attendance poor as the farmers started haymaking on Saturday !"), Hemyock Sunday School treats, baby sitting (Abbey , 1896, ".... in both cases the baby is ill and the mothers being occupied in their dairies cannot attend to sit and so have to keep them at home to do so."), Culmstock Fair, opening of the new Baptist Chapel, farm work (Abbey, 1912, "Father will send him again after the busy time."), potato planting, harvesting and Honiton Fair. Almost in despair, the Abbey teacher wrote, in November, 1903, that "the weather is beautiful so that cannot be blamed. Some are ill but some no excuse." The Dunkeswell Log has two relevant entries for 1934; an intriguing one on 5th May, when a boy "was absent for illegal purposes this afternoon" and, on 29th June, "There are many absences which could be avoided. There are three families which continually give trouble; apart from these, the school would have had an excellent record for attendance." The final entry for the Abbey School, 31st March, 1930, reads, "This School is closed owing to the small attendance."

The Logs also reveal that there were many reasons for official holidays. At the Abbey, there was always a full holiday in September, on the anniversary of the opening of the Church, with two whole days in 1892. There was generally an outing to the sea every year, to Seaton, Sidmouth or Exmouth, and often half holidays for special teas at Wolford Lodge. Other reasons varied; there were the Dunkeswell Club Holidays for several years, with the exasperated comment in 1903 that the Abbey School would stay open and "save giving a holiday as on previous anniversaries of this peculiar rite". The 1893 Royal Wedding, various funerals, Harvest Festival, Ascension Day, the Queen's birthday in 1900 and 1901, Coronation week in 1902, the Abbey choir trip to Seaton, New Year's Day in 1904, Confirmation Day, 1919 Peace celebrations plus an extra week off, the 1922 wedding of Princess Mary, all gained holidays. The last at the Abbey School was on 9th March, 1926, when "Fire (was) discovered in the West roof of the school. Cottagers, with ladders, poured water from buckets on the flames. All fire out and declared safe 11.30 p.m." Telegrams were despatched from Hemyock to the County and the Board of Education and the School was closed for 10th March. Dunkeswell School added a wedding in 1917, Village Sports, the 1919 Strike when the teacher could not get transport to Dunkeswell, the Vicarage Lawn Sale of Work, the 1921 visit to Devon of the Prince of Wales, the use of the premises for the 1922 and 1923 General Elections, the 1923 wedding of the Duke of York, the 1935 Jubilee Service and the wedding of the Duke of Gloucester and Princess Alice, the 1937 Coronation, the outbreak of war in 1939, two days to pick honeysuckle and blackberries in 1941 and the Exeter Pantomime. With so many people absent on so many days, for legal or illegal reasons, perhaps the School Attendance Officer, Mr.Dean, felt quite happy to have volunteered for the Army in France at the end of 1914!

Inspectors were worried, at times. At the Abbey, they found R.I. badly received in 1891, Arithmetic and Geography poor in 1892, pupils rather indifferent in 1893, Arithmetic weak again but Geography good in 1894, the stone floors cold and the closets needing more light and ventilation in 1895, and so on. In Dunkeswell School, in 1921, "There were three boys of the lower group, all dull at learning, but eager enough to attend to other things who had to be reprimanded for inattention by the Inspector", a state of affairs familiar to all teachers. In 1925, "The efficiency of this school is seriously handicapped by the conditions under which the work is at present carried out. The younger children, of whom there are now 23, are taught in the same room as the junior and senior scholars, the numbers totalling 49." The Inspectors said the infants needed a separate class, that there were too many changes of staff, little practical work was done and the infants were restless and disturbed. The room was later divided by a curtain. The Diocesan Inspector was unhappy about the constant changes of Head in 1935.

The HMI were favourably impressed by both Schools on more occasions than they were dissatisfied. At the Abbey, the 1896 report stressed an orderly environment, good work in the upper part of the School and better cloakroom and office accommodation. In later years, "orderly and attentive", "better progress", "under kindly influence and lovingly taught and trained", "the mistress has great control over the children", "this little school is doing very well", "children well behaved, bright and responsive", "children work well unsupervised, orderly, keen, sociable, ready to help", "this remote school is organised with some measure of success", "deep reverence in R.I.", "happy, bright and thoughtful", and, finally in 1929, "good tone in this small school; the visit was a very pleasant one". Dunkeswell School tended to be visited by individual Inspectors regularly but more detailed inspections brought comments such as ,in 1931, "Excellent School. In regard to the top group, it is hard to believe it is the same school I visited a few years ago. First rate work is being done.", and, later, "well conducted", "happy family atmosphere", "encouraging visit and a happy occasion", "happy, interested response", "so conscientiously carried out by the teacher" (Margery Hayman, 1946), and "an alert lot of children who are happy in the work they are doing with their sympathetic teacher" (ditto, 1947); no wonder the children presented a special hairbrush and comb to Miss Hayman when she left to go to Training College in 1948.

The teachers were careful to record disciplinary matters. In 1900, three Abbey boys were "severely cautioned against stone throwing and informed that their parents are liable to a fine of 40/-". One of those boys was in trouble again in 1904; "a boy nearly 14 years of age is exceedingly troublesome with the younger children in the playground, have caned him today, after repeatedly warning him." Another offender, "dishonest in his work", was spoken to "sharply". The whole Abbey School was kept in after school for showing "great disrespect when Rev.W.P.Roberts was speaking" in 1905. In the same year, a boy, "aged 11, showed great impudence this afternoon, his name is entered here, a lasting discredit to his parents". The next year, a boy, "seven years of age, received corporal punishment for using bad language about the school premises, after being warned on previous occasions". Dunkeswell School had just as few problems. In 1919, three children were rebuked for being late; "they cannot be allowed to set all rules at defiance, but nice, well behaved children." In 1935 came a rebuke, tinged with admiration, to some budding cricketers, who had broken a window; "The ball was a wooden one, ingeniously whittled by Jack Evans to take the place of a real cricket ball. The batsman was Rupert Granger." In 1941, "After School today, I, Phyllis M.Riddell, used the birch upon .... for deliberate disobedience and answering back. The boy submitted to the punishment which was given very thoroughly. The rest of the school knew nothing about it", although they probably did the next morning ! In 1942, "I, Phyllis M.Riddell, used the birch after school this afternoon upon .... for persistent disobedience in the singing lesson, the last lesson of the afternoon. He also offended in the morning session, when he tried to push another boy and cause the soiling of many exercise books." Two days later, an eight year old evacuee was birched for misconduct in Church on Ash Wednesday afternoon. Few Dunkeswell girls were ever in trouble, though one was reprimanded in 1917 for "drawing the attention of other scholars to improper writing on the flyleaf of a Reader" and another in 1938, when she and her brother would insist on eating their lunches by the roadside at Deepcut.

Dunkeswell School closed on 27th July, 1949; "School closed. The children will attend Honiton County Primary School next term." Indeed the end of an era which had begun over a hundred years earlier with high hopes for the two schools. Because they were both small and remote schools, the Managers and the County found it hard to appoint Head Teachers and many years were covered with Supply Staff, who always voiced their regret that they were leaving. One temporary Head left in April, 1923, a victim of the post-war depression when the "Geddes Axe" cut public salaries; "I have received notice of dismissal from the Managers .... because I refused to agree to the 5% reduction." So was broken the Parish/School connection in 1949. The Abbey School became a private dwelling, while the Dunkeswell School continued a public life by being turned into the Village Hall. £1,356 was raised to buy the building from the Ministry of Education, which donated £587 to the cause. Ownership of the Hall was vested in the Parish Council, with a separate Management Committee, twelve members representing the Church, Chapel, W.I. and the Cricket Club, with power to co-opt four others. The balance of funds from the old Social Club Committee went to the Hall, which was opened by the Committee Chairman, Alfred Le Marchant, in 1953. Since then, the Hall has been the centre of an active and lively social life for the Parish and, in its opening year, it was used for a Coronation Commemorative Social, the distribution of ration books, a skittling week, committee meetings and private hirings, as for a 21st Birthday party. It must have seemed strange for expupils to return to their old schoolroom but the link with the past has been maintained and appreciated.

Chapter 15

Law and Order

Recalling earlier years in Dunkeswell, a W.I. member said that "everyone went along with the system and you didn't get any terrible trouble" and "any crime was nice crime" and her friends agreed with her. Yet the compiler of Crown Pleas of the Devon Eyre of 1283 wrote, "The countrymen of Devon were aggressive, vindictive, acquisitive and suspicious." What a change there had been over seven hundred years.

The maintenance of law and order in Dunkeswell has always been the responsibility, in the first place, of the local people. In a small community, everyone knew everyone else and that understanding became formalised with the Anglo-Saxon system of Tithings. The village was divided into groups of ten men and those men had a mutual responsibility for the good conduct of the others and their families. If it was believed one had committed a crime, then that person could be Presented to the authorities, either the Lord or a royal official. Under the Normans, the Tithing system was changed to take in larger units and it worked well enough. To assist the enforcement of the law, a Statute of 1285 introduced the Hue and Cry which could be raised on genuine suspicion that a wrongdoer was trying to escape justice and which meant all who heard had to join in the chase after the suspect. It is still law that ordinary citizens should assist Police officers when called upon to do so.

Another step was taken by the Statute of Winchester in 1327, with the creation of the Parish or Petty Constable. Each Parish Constable had a wide range of duties, from arresting suspects and supervising punishments to calling Parish and Vestry meetings and checking that all went to Church on Sundays, and it was a system that lasted until the end of the nineteenth century. It was an unpaid job which went round the village men and, until the seventeenth century, the Parish Constable had to bear all his own expenses; after that, he was entitled to levy a special Rate to cover them. Constables were selected from men who had property or a stake in the village; names of suitable candidates were given to the Lord of the Manor at the Court Leet, later to the Magistrates at Quarter Sessions. Because of the nature of the duties, many tried to avoid being Constable, either by paying another to take over or by lodging a protest. In the 1641 Protestation, Honyball Rawe was written down as the High Constable of Dunkeswell and Andrew Whithorn as the Petty Constable. In 1681, Quarter Sessions said that the Hemyock Hundred Constable, Thomas Barton, should be replaced by either Thomas Marwood or Christopher Searle of Dunkeswell. Twelve years later, Thomas Marwood appeared before the Court to "answer for refusal to be sworn Constable of the Hundred of Hemyock", was discharged and replaced by John Stowhouse and Richard Saroll, both of Dunkeswell. In 1701, it was the turn of Andrew Shapon and John Stephens to do duty. The 1817 Militia Return named Edward Salway as Constable. As late as 1855, Vestry records listed those who could be Constable and whose names were sent to the Justices; they were Francis Clements (Bowerhayes), Robert Burrough (Southlands), Samuel Marks (Pit Place), Thomas Bright (Grange Farm), George Barton (Southey), Samuel Farrant (Connetts), Henry White (Wolford Farm), Roger Rosier, James Webber (Thatcher) and Henry Smith; later additions to the list, up to 1860, were John Banfield (Wolford Farm), James Dimond, William Rosier, John Walker (Musgrove), John Wood, (Hutshayes), John Tucker (Pearsey), John Hardnell (Old Park) and William Baker, (Butcher of Mansells). There is nothing new; there is a Neighbourhood Watch Scheme in the Old Village and there is talk of having Parish Constables, unpaid, once more.

Special Constables could be enrolled in emergencies. In 1847, Bread Riots were feared in Crediton, Cullompton and Tiverton and neighbouring villages might not be immune from some sort of unrest. On 28th May, therefore, the Justices swore in a Dunkeswell man as Special Constable, enjoining him to "well and truly serve our Sovereign Lady the Queen ..... you shall see the Queen's Peace kept, and keep all such watch and ward as are usually accustomed and ought to be kept .... so help you God." His badge of office was a truncheon. Other public spirited men volunteered for Police work as, for example, between 1926 and 1964, when Charles Hayman, Henry Netherway, Edwin Sparks, James Richards, Gilbert Hayman, William Evans, Kenneth Reed, Thomas Canniford, George Stevens, Richard Farrant, Julian

Mountford, Arthur House and Peter Brooke all enrolled as Police Reservists.

During the life of the Abbey, law and order were enforced by the Abbot, who had powers to erect and use gallows on his property and to deal with criminals, and he was kept busy. From 1166, the King sent round his Justices on Eyre (a corruption of itinere, on a journey) and each County Coroner presented pleas to the royal judges. The pleas of 1283 for Dunkeswell began with a murder; William de Schakecumbe had killed Thomas le Chareter and had fled, only to return shortly afterwards to claim sanctuary in Dunkeswell Church. The right to Sanctuary was an old one and no temporal power could forcibly remove anyone from church or churchyard, but immunity from arrest was limited to 40 days. After that time, a criminal either surrendered himself to the King's mercy or, as in the case of William de Schakecumbe, "admitted the deed and abjured the realm before the Coroner"; that is, he swore to leave England, accept banishment and make his way to a designated port, wearing sackcloth but protected by the King's officers. In the same year, the Abbot's Welsh metal founders had killed two of their comrades and fled, the monk had been trapped in the mill wheel at the Abbey, one of the Abbot's men had been crushed to death in a marl pit, though probably at Colaton Raleigh, another had been accused of theft and Reginald Balle had stolen pigs at Buckland Brewer and both had fled and the right of the Abbot to erect gallows on his land had been questioned. Other people were to destroy the Abbot's gallows in Hackpen Manor, use violence against the monks there and drive off Abbey cattle. In 1384, Bywood Grange suffered from a raid by Sir William Asthorpe, Lord of the Manor of Hemyock, who insisted he had rights over Bywood; he and his men drove off cattle and impounded them at Kennerleigh, twenty miles away. The Abbot was so stung by this that he raised an army of 50 local men and retook the cattle, injuring some of the Hemyock men at the pound. Sir William complained to the King but, apparently, nothing happened. After the Black Death, relations between Abbot and other landowners worsened and the Abbot frequently had to go to court to secure his rights. One curious case of 1508 was when there was an alleged assault on the Abbot and Abbey by "diverse wild gentlemen named John Keynes and Umphrey Walronde (who had) gathered a company of riouters to the number of 100 on horseback and on foote, with bows and arrows, bills and other wepens"; the rioters were called before a Court at Cullompton and the matter was investigated by the Bishop of Exeter. However, both the Dunkeswell Abbot and the Forde Abbot, who had been at Dunkeswell on the day concerned, denied that the incident had taken place.

The Abbot's power was taken over by the Justices of the Peace and the Assize Courts and justice was generally done, albeit harshly at times. The value of the system was that the Lords of the Manor of Dunkeswell and the Parish Constables had a good idea of where blame might rest in most reported cases and it was only after the middle of the nineteenth century that changes were made to policing in the County, by the County and Borough Police Act of 1856. Devon Quarter Sessions ordered a Chief Constable be appointed; by 1857, he had recruited 225 policemen and created B District round Honiton. After another seven years, that became D District and it had a Superintendent at Honiton, Sergeants at Honiton, Ottery St.Mary and Axminster, and 28 Constables. The Constables' formal dress of trousers and frock tailed coat, top hat, leather leggings, outside cape and leather haversack, was all black; it gradually became more of an official uniform and helmets were introduced in 1878. Dunkeswell had its own constable, living in what the Census called the Police Station in 1861 and the Constable's Cottage in 1891, next to the School and now called Summerlands. Early photographs show the Devon Constabulary badge above the door, bearing the motto, "Auxilio Divino". The 1923 Wolford Estate sale described it as a "good cottage and garden, with a parlour, kitchen, scullery, two bedrooms, washhouse, fowlhouse and an earth closet", the tenants being the Devon Constabulary. The Police Station moved to what is now the Old Police House, on the main road at Highfield, in 1936.

It is easy to look back at the time of a resident constable as a good time and the Parish Council very much regretted the closure of the Police Station in 1968, following up in 1971 with a resolution that policing from Honiton was inadequate. It is true that a resident constable acted as a deterrent to crime in the village, for he was a Devon man, had a good knowledge of his neighbours and administered some robust justice of his own to lesser transgressors. Yet he had a huge area to cover; the Dunkeswell beat included Luppitt, Beacon, Wick, Sheldon, Combe Raleigh (after 1930) and Upottery (after 1951). It was Dunkeswell's good fortune to be his base. There was a frequent changeover of Constables; some, such as PC Luscombe (1910), PC

Louis Dimond (1902) and the unfortunately named PC Crook (1926), were posted for two year stints. PC John Cann was in Dunkeswell for ten years from 1891, however, and received a subscription from the Parish Council for his good work. In the forty years after 1928, there were 16 different constables in Dunkeswell and only four stayed for over three years 132 George Davies ('39-'43, when he joined the Forces), 73 Arnold Henley ('51-'57), 520 David Hambly ('57-'62) and 792 Eric Rutter ('64-'68).

When the new Beat Books were issued in 1929, the Chief Constable's instructions were that they "must be kept scrupulously clean and always ready for inspection" by the Superintendent and Sergeant and that was what happened, with clear recording of the many aspects which concerned the Constable. Altogether, the entries build up a vivid picture of Dunkeswell, especially the law abiding, good nature of the people. The constable looked after his charges. He went to the scene of domestic accidents, as when Hannah Merchant fell in her bedroom at Rough Grey and broke her arm and Jocelyn Roberts scalded herself at Southayes, both in 1930, when 69 year old George Lake fell in the garden of Woodbine Cottage at Knapp and broke his left leg in 1936 and when the cook at Abbey Meadow Farm was found drunk and incapable on the kitchen floor in 1935. He was called to road accidents, particularly to Percy Hill; Rose Everett went over the handlebars of her bike in 1931, Percy Cousins fell off his bike in 1933, a Flight Sergeant fell from a stationary lorry and dislocated his hip in 1943, there was a fatal fall from a bike in 1949 and the time when 12 year old Leslie Gollop, of Percy Farm, lost control of his bike and ran into a group of people by the bridge, injuring Mrs.Canniford of Garden Cottage in the process. In 1963, a military motor tractor and two trailers failed to take the bend at Southlands Farm and went through the garden wall, injuring 7 Gurkhas from Tidworth. He also attended a nasty accident in 1953, when a motorcyclist received severe injuries after hitting a wandering pig; PC Henley recorded the details, including the identity of those present, and solemnly added "Pig unknown". Falls from horses also occurred; in 1929, Edwin Stevens was thrown from his horse and injured, a Royal Marine Colonel, John Parsons, fell off his horse at Fishponds in 1964, and there was a fatal fall from a pony in 1948. Accidents on the airfield required Police attention, as when a glider cable broke in 1963 and caused serious injury and when a worker fell from a hangar roof on the MOD site in 1956. The Constable also attended meets of the East Devon Hunt at the "Royal Oak" or on neighbouring farms.

Many of the arrests made by constables between 1928 and 1968 were for various road offences, licences, lighting, parking, failure to stop at Halt signs, lack of audible warning on bicycles, etc. Non-payment of domestic rates figured on his list. Dogs were some of the most persistent causes for action, either because they had no licence, were dangerous, bit Rosa Lane of the Forge and George Sanders of Hayne Farm and 17 year old Postwoman Eileen Procter at High Sheldon Farm, were mad, worried sheep at Greenlands Cottage and chicken at Percy Farm and geese at Brookside Farm, strayed on the road, were run over as was Frederick Corrick's "Nigger" by a hit and run driver or knocked Sydney Slade of the "Royal Oak" off his motorcycle in 1933. One RAF wolfhound disgraced itself by killing sheep on the airfield in 1946 and was sent back to the RAF School for Dogs in Gloucester. On the road, dogs would have met horses, cows, sheep, pigs and even a Highwood bull on the loose and livestock being illegally moved, especially in the 1937 Foot and Mouth epidemic. Deaths of chickens from dogs, strychnine poisoning and rats were all part of the work on the beat, as were swine fever at Knapp in 1940 and the overgrown hooves of a 15 year old ass in 1951. Poachers were arrested on the airfield in 1949, having no licences for their shotguns. Thefts were generally on a small scale; in 1929, a pickaxe vanished from Hunters Cottage and firewood from Fishponds, eggs from Abbey fowlhouses in 1931, a car battery from the Wigwam in 1939, daffodils from Dunkeswell Mill in 1953 and lady's knickers from a clothes line in 1956.

High spirits led to a car being pushed into the Slade Farm pond in 1930; less savoury spirits led to anonymous letters and postcards from 1929 to 1934, cautions and fines for the use of obscene language, indecent exposure by a 15 year old from Tiverton which led to three years in an Approved School, a 1940 lorry driver urinating on the highway and a jilted Croydon man pestering a WAAF. The constable attended the scenes of sudden death of children and adults; the 1928-68 Beat Book recorded 14 such incidents, apart from deaths caused by road accidents and accidental shootings.

Constables kept records of Aliens in the Parish, most of whom worked for short periods at Wolford Lodge, and checked their movements. Returns of Gipsies had to be made and their movements noted. The Gipsies were described, named and aged and their vehicles classified. Over the four years from 1929, there were 20 Gipsies on Luppitt Common and one at Wolford; he was Gat Smith from Bristol, born in 1880, 5'6" tall, of dark but cleanshaven complexion and stout, having a Chevrolet motorcycle TT7411. One on Luppitt Common had six children, it was noted, while others were classed as being dirty or very dirty. A few had registered occupations, such as rat catcher, horse dealer, farmer and dealer/labourer. Liberty Hughes lived in a bright yellow caravan pulled by a grey and brown cob, while John Small had a dark, old fashioned caravan with ribbed sides. Hawkers and Pedlars were recorded, one in Dunkeswell being described as a "seller of pegs, brushes, etc.; civil; accompanied by small daughter". Licensed Premises were checked, the names of doctors noted, and motor charabanc, hackney carriage and trade plate owners listed. The Constable went to fires, along with the Honiton Fire Brigade. Some were minor fires, such as the chimney fires at Dunkeswell Grange in 1929, Woodcote bungalow in 1953, Tencery Farm in 1954, Sunnyside Farm in 1955 and Corner Cottage in 1963. There were verge fires, hedge and undergrowth fires and the burning in 1954 of Dunkeswell Common, from a Broadhembury fire. The Manor Farmhouse was destroyed in 1937, when a wooden beam in the sitting room chimney caught alight; it was again a hearth beam that led to the burning down of Brookside Farm in 1938. Little Tencery escaped a similar fate in 1951; Mary Stevens had had some work done by a firm from Honiton and a beam which had been left exposed above the fireplace smouldered for two days before it was seen and damped down. In all, there was little in Dunkeswell that did not come to the notice of the resident constable in his very full working day and he was a reassuring sight to young and old.

Now, Dunkeswell is policed remotely and by the combined Devon and Cornwall Constabulary, in marked contrast with the more personal and direct style of old. It remains, however, a law abiding, low crime rate Parish, the chief targets for criminals being the industrial estate by the airfield and the airfield buildings.

Chapter 16

Parish Administration

Dunkeswell was governed, first of all, by local agents who, in their turn, were supervised by the County and the Crown. The County came under Crown appointees, the Lord Lieutenant and the High Sheriff, although the real work of administration was by the more professional Under-Sheriff, and it lay with these three officials to organise the County for taxation, defence and emergency purposes; they in turn were checked by the Royal Judges. In Dunkeswell, the Lords of the Manor held various courts, such as the Court Leet, which punished minor offences, appointed minor officials and surveyed the behaviour of all within the Manor. View of Frankpledge was another occasion when all the men of the Parish, who had been in residence for a year and a day, presented themselves in their small units before their Lord and accounted for anything amiss; in like manner, there were meetings of the Hundred Court, a Hundred being either a population or land size area, and the Court Baron. The Indenture of 1664, between John Dawe and Nicholas Lyne, both husbandmen of Dunkeswell, and various Citizens of London, stresses the rights of the Lord of the Manor of Dunkeswell, "Liberties Jurisdictions Courts Leets Hundred Courts and Courts Baron", as well as the old medieval rights of "Fairs Markets Tolls Customs Fines Issues Amercements Villeins Bondmen Goods and Chattels of Fugitives and Outlaws Felons of themselves Waifs Strays, etc., etc.", which once covered the rights, or lack of them, of all classes within the Manor. The Lordship of the Manor had been held by the Abbot of Dunkeswell for over 300 years, until 1539. The same rights he had appear in later documents, with a precis of earlier Indentures and agreements. They make painful and tedious reading and one can sympathise with the clerks who wrote out these long documents, especially as each agreement was written out twice on each sheet which was then halved with a jagged or indented cut; in case of any dispute, the two halves were brought together again and it could be seen clearly if any change had been made to one half or the other.

Henry VII (14851509) began to increase the power of the Justices of the Peace and they dealt with virtually every matter within a Parish, especially when they assembled at Quarter Sessions. It has been seen already how they dealt with paupers, bastards, appointment of Constables, apprenticeships, licensing of places of worship, rents and rates; added to those were the setting of wage rates, the price of bread, and many other matters. Roads and bridges came under their jurisdiction; in the Quarter Sessions of 1684, the Magistrates determined the dispute between the Parishioners and Samuel Saroll, who had failed to maintain "a certain common highway lying within the Parish aforesaid over a certain field called Heathland". As the JPs became more powerful, so the powers of the Lord of the Manor decreased, although he was often a JP himself.

Alongside the JPs was the Vestry, which had orginally been when parishioners were called together to discuss Church affairs with the Churchwardens, usually with the system of one man, one vote. No records exist for the early days of the Dunkeswell Vestry but, in the nineteenth century, it was a fairly select and unelected body of the bigger farmers. Records do exist from 1850 to 1875; in 1850, the Chairman and senior Churchwarden was Robert Burrough, of Mansells, and there were twelve other ratepayers (of £10 or more assessment), men such as John Clements of Bowerhayes and William Tucker of Percy Farm. Later that year, Joseph Burrows took the Chair. In the twenty five years of its records, the Vestry was an entirely male affair, except that Mrs.Anne Burrough became an Overseer of the Poor in 1873. It met on the Thursday after the Sunday, when a convening notice had been placed on the Church door and a copy on the "Chaple". Each year, the members elected their Chairman, two Churchwardens (the other in 1850 was Robert Smith of Tencery Farm), two Overseers of the Poor (William Chinnick and Francis Clements) and a Surveyor of the Highway (Francis Clements of Whitehorns) and declared a rate for the year. The Vestry was aided in its deliberations by the Parish Clerk (Edward Salway). There may have been a separate Vestry for Dunkeswell Abbey as Billing's Directory for 1857 names T.Richards as the Abbey Clerk; the Dunkeswell Vestry, however, appeared to include the Abbey in its decisions. The Vestry saw to the upkeep of the churchyard wall and the welfare of the poor, the rebuilding of the Church and the new school. The members met in the Parish Room, by

Corner Cottage, as did their successors, and much time was taken up with discussing repairs to the building, especially stopping the leaks in the roof and walls, rethatching the roof and rebuilding the chimney. Exactly the same problems were inherited by the Parish Council and it even had to take legal advice when Mrs.Middleton, of Corner Cottage, constantly held the Council responsible for the water that leaked into her house; the dispute lasted several years and took up much time, until the two parties reached a compromise.

One special task of the Vestry was to deal with the roads in the Parish. A 1763 map of Devon, by Benjamin Donn of Bideford, fails to show any direct road to Dunkeswell, access being via Luppitt and Hembury Fort. The Rev.Mr.Swete had not been impressed by the rough road from the Abbey but it had been the duty of the Surveyor of Highways, until 1835, to set the Parishioners to work to repair such highways as there were and small bridges over the Madford. The appointment was passed round each year and was not a popular one; if a reluctant Surveyor could pay some one else to do the job, then he often did so. Each Surveyor had to chivy his neighbours into providing labour, material or transport, under the Highway Act of 1555, for six days a year. Because no one liked the task, the Surveyor found it hard going; he was rarely an expert and the work was often skimped, in time and material, so roads were badly maintained. At least, there was always somewhere to dump the stones and flints that kept rising to the surface of the fields. Even Turnpike Roads, such as the one from Honiton to Taunton via Limers Cross, had to have labour in addition to that paid for by the Turnpike Trust itself from the various tolls it collected. After 1835, the post of Surveyor of Highways still had to be filled, until the end of the century, but the work was much lighter and really consisted of keeping a check on road faults and surfaces, a task still being done by Parish Councillors. Some of those appointed after Francis Clements were Henry White, William Broom, John Thomas Banfield, Thomas Derham, John Tucker and Samuel Marks.

Under the Local Government Act of 1894, the Vestry was replaced by the Parish Council, elected then by ratepayers, now by all on the Electoral Register, although electors did not necessarily have much interest in what was done in their name. In a meeting in the Schoolroom in 1949, Chairman Henry Canniford regretted that "there was little interest by Parishioners in Council affairs". No one at all attended the 1961 meeting, although, presumably, the Clerk was there, the Chairman being ill, and the Rev.William Williams's last Annual Meeting in 1965 conducted no business as there were so few there. Despite that, Council Chairmen were mainly long-serving and there were only thirteen of them in the first hundred years. Samuel Kittow was in office for nearly twenty years from 1894, Henry Canniford fifteen years from 1938, James Griffin Farmer thirteen years from 1918 and Alan Ralph eleven years from 1972. That the nature of Council business has changed in intensity and pressure is shown by the fact that Samuel Kittow chaired 59 meetings (average per annum 3) while Alan Ralph chaired 111 (10).

Undoubtedly, Council business can be monotonous and frustrating but it reveals much about the way a village lives. In general, the Council aimed to keep and improve the standard of life within the Parish and to remove anything that might have gone against it. It tried to maintain housing availability by preserving houses and filling empty ones, although it did express its indignation at the Department of Social Security in 1970, when the DSS sent the occupants of the Old Police House on holiday while the house was repaired and cleaned, condemning it as "a frivolous use of tax and rate payers' money". Before the end of the first War, it was asking for housing for its people and, eventually, gained Broomfield (originally Hillside), Abbey Road, Springfield and the old people's bungalows in Abbey Road. The Council also allowed private building and conversion of existing buildings, as in the Tencery Farm area.

The Parish Council looked at plans for development by outsiders, from the Godmanstone plans in 1973 through to those of Westward Developments for Highfield, with comments in 1975 on the proposed Playing Field, Village Hall, Clinic, Library, Car Park, Shopping Area, Primary School and improved roads. It watched the Bithrey site by the Royal Oak from 1985 and various attempts to create caravan parks at Blossom Hill in 1979, at Southayes in 1968 and on the airfield in 1974. It did its best to get rid of unwanted dwellers, such as the squatters on the airfield, whose sanitary arrangements were denounced in 1951, and those on the Turbury, who created mess and smells in 1973; such travellers proved troublesome again in the 1990s. It supported special occasions; there was a donation towards the Devon fund for the Diamond Jubilee of Queen Victoria in 1898 and £5 to the 1935 Jubilee

Committee, which purchased the commemorative seat placed near the Forge. It gave permission for the ladies to have a house-to-house collection for the Princess Elizabeth Fund in 1947, refused to do anything special for the Festival of Britain in 1951 but gave money and help to the 1953 Coronation Committee, the year in which it repainted the Jubilee seat. Queen Elizabeth's Silver Jubilee in 1977 was deemed worthy of the distribution of 140 Jubilee mugs to the under-16s in the Parish.

Footpaths and bridleways were always on the agenda. The longest running saga of these was Bridleway 12, from 1973, when it was proposed that the Bridleway be retained; in 1981, the minutes read, "Bridleway 12 is becoming urgent". Two meetings later, there was what the Footpath Warden stated; "Everything that could be done in respect of Bridleway 12 would be done at an early date." That early date proved to be 1993 ! Other paths were checked; repeated requests to the owner of the Mill pond to clear the footpath by it were unavailing. In the end, the Council paid for the clearance to be done and charged the owner, in 1961, although that did not stop the dumping of rubbish in the stream from 1957 to 1963, when a feet-dragging Rural District Council reluctantly agreed to two rubbish collections each month. Mr.Burrough was asked to clear a dangerous wall by Precious Court in 1900, Mr.Dare was reminded of the dangerous state of the footpath by the Mill pond in 1908, it was hoped all 3rd class roads should be rolled and repaired as soon as possible and the Sheepwash and Brookside bridges be repaired in 1925, and Mr.Burrows was asked to remove obstructions by Bottom Cottage in 1933. The Council promised to walk and inspect all paths and "rightaways" in 1950, accepted Laurie Churcher's complaint about the state of the path and road outside his house at Knapp in 1953, and nagged away in the 1960s and 1970s until the rubble from the collapsed 1 Church Terrace was carted away after exposure on television. In 1964, the lane to Mansells was reported to be so bad that tradesmen refused to deliver to the house.

The Council pressed for the installation of electricity and water and a proper sewage system in the post2nd War years. The USN had had electricity on the airfield, as had had the RAF wireless station at Wolford; the Police House was attached to the supply before the War ended but it was not until 4th August, 1953, that the main village supply was switched on by the Rector's wife, Mrs.Vokes. Basic street lighting was not to come until 1975; even then, it had been rejected in 1970 and there were dark gaps by the Village Hall and Corner Cottage. Water, too, had gone to the Americans and gradually had come into the old village. From 1959, the Council had been pressing for a main sewage system, spurred on by strong smells from the areas of the Rectory and Connetts Farm, with complaints about the Royal Oak in 1969, a fault which was finally remedied by the Brewers the following year.

Pollution worried the Council, especially that from the industrial units by the airfield, the worst offender being Kay's Transport from 1979, and the slurry from Westerhope; slurry and whey were also dumped on the airfield and it took a long struggle to get recognition of the facts of pollution of the watercourses. Visual nuisances were tackled, one of the worst being the scrapheaps on Percy Hill and Highfield, against which the Dunkeswell W.I. protested to the Council in 1969, the first of many complaints. The council was concerned about the amount of noise that came from the airfield, from the Kart racing from 1965 onwards. It also was horrified at the huge crowd that appeared to watch Drag Racing in 1971, some 13,000 people and 4,000 cars; local people threatened a planned closure of approach roads, with tractors and farm equipment, should the Drag Racing be allowed to go on. There was another outburst of protest in the 1980s, against the proposed, large scale car racing and testing and a leisure complex on the airfield; in the face of such widespread condemnation, the plans were dropped. In the 1990s, there was worry about possible Rave parties on the airfield, with strong action being taken by the Police.

In 1953, the Council met in the old School, which had become a Village Hall vested in the Council. It was a relief that the old and faulty Parish Room should be sold in 1968 for £205, enabling a store to be erected at the Village Hall for £100 in the same year. Not that there was a great deal of Council property to store; an inventory of the Parish Room in 1920 was very brief - 6 long forms, 4 short forms, 2 seats with backs, 2 tables, 1 bagatelle board with frame and balls complete, 3 pictures, 1 writing desk, 1 King board, a platform with trestles and "boxes with contents". A rather mysterious minute of a 1946 meeting, referring to some Council property, read, "Mrs. .... must bring the fountain back to the Parish Room, clean and in good condition."

Another long running discontent was the refusal of the Government departments to re-open the road over the airfield and the council was intensely niggled by its lack of progress in the post-War years; the Clerk was to write many a letter to the RDC, County Council and Whitehall, thus earning his remuneration. The earliest reference to a salary for the Clerk was in 1927, when the figure was £2 per annum, rising to £2.10.0 in 1934, £4 in 1949 and £5 in 1958, and an interesting record appeared in 1935, which would seem to allow payments in kind for the Clerk; in that year he had obviously done some extra work with regards to the Parish Room and it was agreed that he should be given the stones from the old chimney as a reward.

The Council checked the accident blackspots at School and Deepcut corners and the possible danger of the bank below the road at Sunnybank, tried to secure more than one bus a week to Honiton in 1959 and allowed adults on the school bus, until that became too overcrowded and it had to ask for a second bus in 1967; it checked that Common Land at Gypsy Cross and the Turbury was registered in 1967, campaigned for a speed limit within the old village, approved SW Water's new water tower and checked water quality and pressure and was sympathetic to post-War moves to establish some sort of Defence Force in 1980. In 1899, it had responded to a letter from Churchstanton Council, pledging its support for a light railway from Hemyock to either Ilminster or Chard, of which no more was heard.

It kept an eye on the Post Office, in part of the late seventeenth century complex of Bankside and Spring Cottages; Census records and Devon Directories name the Postmasters and the times of post arriving and departing, with modifications being requested by the Parish Council. In 1857, Edward Salway was Dunkeswell Postmaster and post arrived at 8.30 a.m. and departed at 3.45 p.m. Thomas Salway later took over; he was aged 74 in 1891 and was later replaced by Harry George Clode, still there in 1939. Then came the Vestys, Malcolm and Daphne Andrews and Peter and Toni Wagstaffe. The Post Office itself was strong in the memories of US personnel and it lends a charm to the old village, with its thatch and garden and warm welcome for all. The Abbey also had postal services and letters there came via Exeter, Honiton, Cullompton and Wellington, which must have been confusing for all. In pre-2nd War Dunkeswell, the postman used to walk out from Honiton, then rest in a shed by the present Bithrey site or do odd jobs

A 1930's view of Dunkeswell from Percy Hill

The Post Office

until it was time for him to walk back to Honiton with the outgoing post. In 1908, Dunkeswell Post Office could open at 8.00 a.m. instead of 7.00, and in 1931 the Dunkeswell Postman was to have a Saturday half-day, with the Abbey following in 1937. The Mail Bus, one of the first in the country, started to serve Dunkeswell in October, 1968, carrying between 20 and 30 passengers a week and taking 50/-; it is a sad thought that present threats of privatisation of the Post Office might end such postal and social work.

In all, it was a busy Parish Council; the only recorded rebuke to its members was when the Rev.William Williams, 1964 Chairman, stated that all future decisions would be taken by secret ballot, as there had been a leakage of information from within the Council over the years. Today, the Council is always in open session and there is a slot for questions from members of the public, the secret ballot used only for the election of the Chairman and officers.

Chapter 17

Conclusion

In so many ways, the history of Dunkeswell has mirrored and fitted into the general history of England; in others, the village has maintained its sturdy independence, remote from transitory fashions and tendencies. Even now, it may look at the many newcomers and their ways and still keep to its traditional way of life; it is still bound by the passing seasons and the elements, tight family groupings and a strong sense of duty to the community. There are no great houses or suburban streets within the village or at the Abbey but a happy co-existence of all sorts of people, brought together by a lively awareness of the good and valuable things of life. The Church may no longer be the centre of village life but it still figures high on the list of fixed points in the complexity of modern life. The Rector may not be the combined spiritual leader and comforter, social worker, charity dispenser, enforcer of moral law and order and general overseer of village life, but he and his family are still in the Rectory, available at all hours and for all reasons, in sad times and in happy times, for families and for individuals, being within the Parish and not simply within the Church of England. The village policeman may have quit his house but there is still an innate respect for the law of the land. History does bind us all, whether we fully appreciate it or not, and gives us a base from which to advance.

BIBLIOGRAPY

Various sources in the Devon Record Office and the Westcountry Studies Library, Castle Street, Exeter, and documents on loan from Mr.Peter Luscombe, Wolford Farm.

K.Barker and R.Kain Maps and History in S.W.England 1991 Exeter Studies in History No.31

J.Blome Placenames of North Devon 1929 Uppsala

S.H.Bull The Queen's York Rangers 1984

S.H.Burton Devon Villages 1973 Robert Hale

P.Caraman The Western Rising, 1549 1994 Westcountry Books

B.Cherry and N.Pevsner Devon 1989 Penguin (Buildings of England series)

T.Clare Archaeological Sites of Devon and Cornwall 1982 Moorland

J.R.W.Coxhead Honiton 1984

The Countryside Commission The Blackdown Hills Landscape 1989

Devon Federation of W.I.s Within Living Memory 1993 Countryside Books/W.I.

F.J.Donaldson The Fatal Echo 1990 WRGI

M.Edmunds Honiton 1993 Westcountry Books

M.B.Fryer Elizabeth Posthuma Simcoe 1989 Toronto

J.Gover, A.Mawer, F.Stenton Placenames of Devon CUP

A.Grigg Place Names in Devon and Cornwall 1988 Plymouth

W.G.Hoskin Devon 1972 David and Charles

W.G.Hoskin Old Devon 1966

W.G.Hoskin The Making of the English Landscape 1955 Hodder and Stoughton

W.J.Hutchings Out of the Blue 1956

R.Love The Blackdown Hills 1993 Blackdown Hills Project

R.Muir Reading the Landscape 1981 Shell

J.R.Robertson The Diary of Mrs.John Graves Simcoe 1911 Toronto

I.Roots The Monmouth Rising 1986 Devon Books

R.R.Sellman Aspects of Devon History 1985 Devon Books

R.J.Silvester An Excavation at Dunkeswell 1980 Devon Archaeological Society

J.A.Sparks In the Shadow of the Blackdowns 1978 Moonraker
R.Stanes A History of Devon 1986 Phillimore
R.Stanes The Old Farm 1990 Devon Books
J.M.Stratton Agricultural Records, 220-1977 1979 John Baker
J.Sturt Revolt in the West 1987 Devon Books
M.Todd The South-West to AD 1,000 1987 Longmans
E.Walford War over the West 1989 Amigo
R.Webber The Devon and Somerset Blackdowns 1976
S.Wheeliker and S.Eyles Poor Relief in Devon 1991 Devon Association
J.Whiles Sedgemoor 1985 Picton
H.J.Yallop Honiton and the Otter Valley 1992 Alan Sutton
H.J.Yallop The Honiton Lace Industry 1992 UEP

Index